WHAT PEOPLE ARE SAYING ABOUT

CARRY THE ROCK

Carry the Rock is a poignant look at the process of spiritual birth – from the perspective of the apprentice emerging, often painfully, into a new world which extends far beyond the unanticipated limitations of one's teacher. The personal anecdotes are revealing and instructive and it is clear that Jessica made the leap to Freedom long before she realized it herself. As readers, we are blessed that she has taken the time to write of the good, the bad and the ugly which inevitably arise on the rocky road toward the evolution of a truly infinite Spirit.

Della Van Hise, author of *Quantum Shaman: Diary of a Nagual Woman*

Carry the Rock

An Apprentice Journey

Carry the Rock

An Apprentice Journey

Jessica D. Rzeszewski

MOON BOOKS

Winchester, UK
Washington, USA

First published by Moon Books, 2014
Moon Books is an imprint of John Hunt Publishing Ltd., Laurel House, Station Approach, Alresford, Hants, SO24 9JH, UK
office1@jhpbooks.net
www.johnhuntpublishing.com
www.moon-books.net

For distributor details and how to order please visit the 'Ordering' section on our website.

ISBN: 978 1 78279 765 4

A CIP catalogue record for this book is available from the British Library.

Design: Stuart Davies
www.stuartdaviesart.com

Printed in the USA by Edwards Brothers Malloy

CONTENTS

Prologue

The Nagual asked for a volunteer. Linda raised her hand. We stood in a circle underneath a monkeypod tree in a state park on the far side of the island. We were a circle of apprentices, studying with a leader in the Toltec tradition called a Nagual. The Nagual is a conduit to knowledge that leads one to recognize the unseen in the world and to merge what we know with things we don't know. The lesson that day was to gain the ability to recognize energy in ourselves and in those around us.

"I want you to lie down; close your eyes," the Nagual instructed Linda.

Linda lay prone on the grass, and the Nagual kneeled down, placing her hands palms up underneath her left shoulder.

"The rest of us will place our hands in the same fashion."

The remaining seven women shifted slightly to form a tight circle around Linda, and placed their hands underneath her.

"Now lift her up," the Nagual instructed, "to here," indicating for us to lift Linda to elbow height as she stood up and held her forearms straight out from her hips. Linda's eyes flew open at hearing the Nagual's instructions and she giggled. Several women laughed with a nervous twitter and gaped at the Nagual as though she were daft. "Go ahead, do it," she instructed, nonplussed.

Turns out it wasn't as difficult as most of us imagined it would be, nor as strenuous. We lifted Linda, who was quite petite, into the air as though she were a fragile patient being transferred from a paramedic gurney to a hospital bed. At the moment of our collective sigh, the Nagual instructed, "Now turn your palms and drop all fingers except one on each hand." Everyone adjusted to the new directive, and there was a second sigh as Linda remained in the air with only a motley crew of single digits holding her up.

"What are we doing?" the Nagual prompted the group.

"We're challenging the idea of what we think we can achieve," said Suzanne. Her response was assured but her tone carried an inkling of doubt.

"We're following directions," said Carol, who loved to counter the Nagual's directness by sidestepping the issue (yet always in a way that couldn't be faulted), as though she knew what the Nagual expected to hear and she wasn't going to be the one to give it.

"We're scaring the hell out of Linda?" ventured another. All of the women laughed, including Linda, although her giggle cut short. "You guys are moving me!" Alarmed that the laughter caused our finger positioning to shift her body ever so slightly, Linda held still as a statue.

"Now close your eyes. I want you to feel the energy as you continue to hold Linda in the air. Tell us what you feel." The Nagual was moving into the heart of the lesson. The group grew pensive, feeling whatever it is one feels when directed to "feel the energy." Images popped onto my mental screen. I saw a plumeria blossom, an aromatic flower used in Hawaiian leis. The feeling was lighthearted, a breeze that carried a sweet scent. Linda was no burden to hold up; she was a new member to the group, curious and respectful to those around her, eager to learn about the Nagual's teachings.

Each woman had the opportunity to be carried by the group. One woman declined. One woman was on the heftier side, and I assure you, all of us wondered whether or not we'd be able to lift her with our little collection of single digits. Each woman's energy was different. Some, like Linda, were buoyant and carefree; some were dense and even dark, while some were playful, reaching out in order to connect to those in the circle. I wondered what my energy was like. Once we were all seated on the ground, the Nagual continued the lesson.

"Carry the rock, not the weight of the rock," she said, eyeing the group, challenging us with her glance to make the connection between the koan and our recent experience. "How is it that everyone felt different?" she queried, "and I'm not talking about a difference in pounds here." The Nagual looked pointedly at Carol before she could utter a word. The discussion continued as the group talked about differences in energy, what it felt like to carry another's energy, and the experience of muddied energy as opposed to a clear, direct exchange.

I was transfixed. I had been wondering for some time how much of my relationship with the Nagual related to my purpose for being an apprentice or more to a discomfort in the relationship with her that left me feeling like I was perpetually launched halfway over a hurdle hanging in midair. How much of my relationship with the Nagual was free and clear, and how much of it was "all in a wad" because of the weight that had been attributed to it?

Preface

It has been more than five years now since I finished writing the account of my apprenticeship with the Nagual. At the time the story hadn't set right with me, and I had put it away. The Nagual told me that she herself had written about her apprenticeship with her teacher, but then she'd purposefully edited out those experiences that put her teacher in a bad light. There had been plenty to include had she felt inclined to reveal that side of her teacher, but in the end she'd concluded there was no purpose to such exposure; she wanted to convey only those experiences that would highlight the positive.

I pondered this perspective for a long while. It sounded respectful and judicious. If she'd taken that stance in telling her story, it simply wouldn't do for me to speak of my apprenticeship with her otherwise. I should be respectful and judicious, too. And the result was that the story sat on a shelf.

That story was over and done with, and so I moved on to other aspects of my journey. I became immersed in writing *Encounter with Power: A Journey from the Toltec Perspective*,[1] a story about stepping into the power of who I am in relationship to what confronts me. At every juncture of my journey I was learning that there were things to hold on to and things to let go of, even though the difference between the two wasn't always as clear as I wanted it to be. And so without feeling totally aware of why, the story of my apprenticeship was never completed. I had set the weight of it down, or so I thought.

I'm not implying that something mysterious was happening in relation to the story. If there was, I was clueless to it. What I'm saying is that the death of my involvement with the story is precisely what allowed it to be resurrected. I'd set it aside because I'd needed it to die. I had needed to move away from my experience because the weight of it was too heavy. Resurrection was not in the equation until I realized that the story had potency separate from my weighty involvement with it.

One day it was simply time to start writing again. I pulled the manuscript out while looking for reference material on another topic. Good God almighty, I hadn't read the story in five years! Yet it gripped me as I reread it. How many apprentices had had similar experiences and not talked about it? How many stories had been written with "happy endings" and didn't allow for ambiguity or indecision or lack of clarity in the last chapter's end line? Sure, cliffhangers keep the readers' eyes focused at the end of each chapter, but at the end of the book? Readers want it wrapped up nice and neat, no messy endings, please! I want to challenge the assumption that a good story concludes with all of the ends tied together and the lesson learned. That's not always the way life unfolds, and a good story doesn't require a storybook ending. Readers can draw their own conclusions and walk away from the story with an ending unique to themselves.

The five-year lapse allowed me to see what I couldn't see at the time – while still carrying the weight of the story – because I'd wanted the storybook ending with such an intensity that I'd been blinded to what had actually occurred. What had occurred was an apprentice experience with a Nagual who taught me exactly what I needed for that moment in my life. I came to recognize that while my experience may be familiar to many apprentices, the conclusions drawn from such an experience either propel the apprentice forward or become a barrier that waylays the journey. The journey continues only when that hurdle is cleared without it becoming a stumbling block. My story is worth telling, warts and all, for the many apprentices who have had a similar experience and are unsure of how to continue their journey to freedom.

My apprenticeship was a quest for freedom. In the Toltec tradition, "freedom" means gaining a point of view in daily life free from preconceived ideas, values, beliefs, and emotions.

Freedom means approaching life with a balance between the "Tonal" and the "Nagual."

The Tonal represents everything we see, everything we know, and everything we understand. It is daily life viewed through our eyes and our hearts without any filters that influence the experience.

The Nagual, on the other hand, represents everything we do not see, everything that is unknown to us, and everything experienced through our bodies (both physical and etheric), including our souls. It is the mysterious in the world that oftentimes can't be seen. To attain freedom in the Toltec tradition is to merge these two worlds into one without duality.

This story is not told with the sole purpose of emphasizing the Nagual's teachings, although they are included throughout the story. However, the story places equal emphasis on the interactions that took place between the Nagual and myself throughout my apprenticeship, because it is oftentimes these interactions that can easily bog an apprentice down, causing his or her journey to end in defeat or discouragement.

Remember Dorothy's journey in *The Wizard of Oz*? Dorothy was lost, although she had the wherewithal to return home by using her ruby slippers from the outset of her journey. She hadn't known she had her own resources to complete her journey home. She had faced challenges throughout her travels on the Yellow Brick Road, but she hadn't been successful in returning to Kansas until she realized she'd had the means to return home all along. Long before she pulled the curtain back from the mighty Oz and exposed his humanness, she'd had the wherewithal to end her journey – she just hadn't known it – and neither did I at the outset of my journey. My story is the journey from "not knowing" to "knowing," just as was Dorothy's in the Land of Oz.

The journey I tell is in four sections, each one comprising of one of the four directions: West, North, East, and South. In shamanism, the four directions are pictured as four quadrants of a medicine wheel. The participant using the medicine wheel as a tool for growth has the opportunity to evolve, to mature, and to develop non-duality through events in their lives that present them with challenge, whether a problem to be solved, an issue to understand and assimilate, or an experience that furthers their appropriation of life on a daily basis. Each section outlined in the book propels me through experiences that highlight the significance of that direction.

Non-duality and freedom are two terms the reader will come across throughout the book. Freedom is described in previous paragraphs. The definition for non-duality is to live in the present moment such that there is nothing to compete with, compare to, or contrast against the very moment being experienced. There is only one moment and that moment is now. In addition, non-duality is the experience of oneness with all that is available, internally and externally, bringing together the disparate events in our lives into a unified, energetic whole with little emphasis on the past or on the future.

The story opens with an emphasis on the West, including a physical move west from California to Hawaii. The West direction is a look within to the intellectual aspect of who one is. As I moved from California to Hawaii I brought with me few physical belongings; although in contrast, I brought with me loads of ideas and beliefs about freedom and its composition. These were in direct contrast to many religious ideas and beliefs I was in the process of letting go of, after many years of living in a church environment. I knew I hadn't arrived at freedom, but I had a good idea how to get there. The West is the direction of endings and letting go. Little did I know how weighty my ideas and beliefs were, and how difficult it would be to let them go.

The North emphasizes the mental arena with wisdom as the desired outcome. Before the apprentice can move into his or her own wisdom, a period of discomfort and hardship awaits them. My discomfort wasn't due to physical elements but to those mental and relationship issues that dogged my apprenticeship, as my preconceived ideas about what an apprenticeship would be clashed with what was actually unfolding.

The East brings illumination, just as in the dawning of a new day. It is the direction of gaining awareness. As I grappled with differences in language usage between the Nagual and myself, a misunderstanding of relationship cues, and a lack of clarity in the Nagual's teachings, I began to draw upon sources for illumination that I hadn't expected to influence me during the apprenticeship.

The South is the place of innocence and trust. Placing trust in who we are allows for growth and reliance upon all life to provide the wherewithal for our maturity. I expected my growth to be generated from the Nagual and her teachings because she was the expert. What I experienced, however, was that expertise comes from unexpected places, and it is when the apprentice develops trust in her own wisdom, rather than placing it in someone else, that freedom can take flight.

Part One: West

– The direction of Death, signifying endings, the place of letting go. West also symbolizes water, emotions, the psyche, movement, and introspection.

The sun surrenders itself into the ocean each evening as the day comes to an end and moves into the black of night.

September 16

It was late in the evening before my morning flight, as I arranged what little bedding I had on the floor in the bedroom. One more night of sleeping on the floor, and in the morning I would hand over the condo keys to the couple that were to become its new occupants. I smiled, picturing them the day they had walked through the condo, a young couple with no children and, by the looks they had exchanged between them, still in love with each other and with life. They were the tenants I'd been hoping to find.

To say I was excited is an understatement, although to say I was exhausted can't be overstated. I'd never made a move of such geographical distance and my fingers were crossed that I wouldn't miss anything. Only recently had my divorce been finalized, from my husband of twenty years who happened to be the pastor of a church. This change in my life was large enough to negotiate on its own, but an even bigger change was letting go of so many of the beliefs that had come with having been involved in the church as the pastor's wife. I was leaving a lifetime of religious beliefs behind me. Over the two years previous, I'd also adopted a new set of beliefs in the form of shamanism.

My "move to Hawaii" list was checked complete as of 11:40pm that evening, including the release of spiritual ideologies and physical items that had comprised my life for so many years. The move had taken six months to orchestrate, and what a relief to have it almost over with.

The previous three weeks had been chaotic: ending employment, painting the interior of the condo, finding renters, putting what little belongings I had into a crate heading across the Pacific Ocean, and seeking a new family to take Tawny, our cat. Everything I owned was either on a freighter or stuffed into the suitcase lying next to me in the empty room.

It was down to the wire; my flight was the next day at eleven in the morning, which meant getting to John Wayne Airport by nine. Sleep couldn't come soon enough. I closed my eyes, and, blessedly, sleep arrived the moment my head hit the rolled-up towel I was using as a temporary pillow.

There was no clock on the nightstand to announce the time, but I awoke to the feeling of Tawny walking along my back. How odd! That meant she had found her way home from across town and entered the condo. She must have come through the open patio door. Quiet exhilaration filled me. Ah! She'd made it home. How we loved our cat! We'd given her to a Craigslist family looking for a cat, because it hadn't made sense to put her into the quarantine required by the state of Hawaii. That had been a few weeks ago, as my daughters and I had stood on the second story patio overlooking the carport, crying and sniffling as we watched Tawny's new family drive away with her. They had promised to give her as much love as we'd given her, and we had believed them.

The day after that, my daughter Carla had flown to New York, and a day later my other daughter, Laurelle, had flown to Hawaii, both of them to start fall semester at college. I had remained behind a few extra weeks to close up the remaining details of our life in Orange County, CA. As a family we'd lived in this area for the previous twenty years, so it was a monumental change for all of us to be moving to different areas of the country and adopting new ways of approaching life.

"Wait a minute!" I thought. "Tawny's new family lives in Anaheim. That is quite a distance for a house cat to travel. In fact, quite an improbable distance to return all the way to Tustin, across concrete jungle, suburban sprawl, and a dozen criss-crossed freeways. Impossible for a cat, really."

Suddenly aware that I am dreaming, I turn to Stephanie in the dream and whisper, breathlessly, "Look on my back. Tell me what's there."

Stephanie is a dream character that often shows up as a guide and comrade in arms while dreaming. She doesn't always speak, but whenever I'm backed against the wall, she always "has my back." In this dream, I struggled as though forcing the words out of my mouth.

In the dream, Stephanie's eyes open wide like an aperture on a camera, as does her mouth. "It's a cat!" she cries. Her comment leaves me at the exact corner where I am already standing.

My dreaming practices had started two years previous when I had begun to read Carlos Castaneda, a shaman who practiced in the Toltec tradition. In that practice, the use of nighttime dreaming was highly regarded as a means of uniting two disparate ways of being in the world: the Tonal (what can be seen) and the Nagual (what is unseen).

Finally cognizant that I am dreaming, I turn to my left and open a single eye stealthily so as not to awaken from the dream. If I could for one brief moment look at the cat, I'd know in a split second whether or not it was Tawny. "No!" I think. "It's not Tawny's red and white head, with those large copper eyes she'd had since tumbling out of a corner of Laurelle's closet weeks after her birth." Instead, the ears of this cat in the dream are jet black, as is the head. A cat, all right, though not a tabby house cat. The green eye looking back at me is far from domesticated. This black panther is purring as it sits on top of me, breathing in rhythm with the scratchy movement of a tongue on a forepaw.

Suddenly, a second animal enters my awareness. Turning my head warily to the right, I open my other eye. Hanging over my shoulder is the massive yellow head of a lion, without a mane, its body also positioned tidily on top of me. I sense the lion is young, innocent, and unproven in a scrimmage. The staggering weight of the two animals on my back suddenly becomes unbearable. It doesn't occur to me that two full-grown wild cats can't possibly fit on my one hundred and thirty pound frame. Both of them are calm. They aren't going anywhere. In fact, they've shown up on my behalf. Suddenly, I know they are there as guardians to my journey across the Pacific.

As the dream faded away, I fell back asleep feeling greatly comforted.

September 20

The hygienist's words were haunting me as I lay on the single bed at the Honolulu YMCA, my face buried in a lumpy pillow with a distinct smell of antiseptic. "It looks like it'll need a root canal soon," she'd said. "The decayed portion is almost to the nerve. No telling what the dentist will uncover when he drills, sweetie, and he won't have a chance to do anything about it today." Thirty minutes later, the dentist had filled my cavity, but the tooth in question had been left untouched. "Let's schedule you next week to take a look at it," the dentist had suggested.

But that second dental appointment had never taken place because two days later I'd flown to Hawaii, and there I was again, in bed, trying to deal with the pain in my left molar, which wouldn't let up. I hadn't eaten much of anything for days, and Tylenol wasn't putting a dent in the throb coming from my jaw.

All day I'd looked at rentals in the Honolulu area without any luck. When a rental agent said, "Why don't you drive by that location first and then give me a call," it didn't take long to catch on that we would no more want to live at those locations than we wanted to continue our stay at the YMCA.

Back at the Y, I glanced over at my daughter, Laurelle. Her nose was buried in a textbook, and she was scribbling notes on a notepad. She had arrived nearly a month prior to start the fall semester, and she was already knee-deep in homework.

A few of the long-term residents had challenged her idea of the not-so-clear line between sanity and insanity. "Frightened her" would be a more apt description. Normally outgoing and gregarious, Laurelle invited conversation easily with those around her. But in the three weeks she had been waiting for me to arrive, she'd had plenty of wacky conversation with other residents standing in the cafeteria line that had left her shaken. She'd gained a new appreciation for what it would be like to live at the Y, either by choice or from necessity. Both depressed her. It was crucial that she live close to the university campus, but those places not requiring a drive-by disclaimer had been scooped up weeks prior to the start of the fall semester.

I was weary-to-the-bone tired, and I'd looked at every listing in the paper for available rentals. The next day would be a trip downtown to Kinko's for rental listings online.

"How's your tooth, Mom?" Laurelle asked, looking up from her reading.

"… hurts," I mumbled and closed my eyes. A conversation at that moment about much of anything felt futile.

"Did you get hold of Carla?" she asked.

I nodded a slow no. That conversation, too, would leave me feeling an utter sense of helplessness. She'd been trying to figure out housing arrangements, class schedule, buying of textbooks – all of those things a first year college student does – on her own in New York City. She felt light years away.

Ten years with no major dental work, and then a few days after moving to Hawaii a tooth blows out. Control over my decisions felt like it was slipping through my fingers. Thoughts swirled through my pounding head in time with the throbbing molar: *No dental insurance until I get a job. A job won't come for another six weeks. Emergency dental care is too expensive. This move has been way more costly than I expected. Use a credit card for the dental work, for God's sake!*

Pressing my cheek against the pillow, I opened my weary eyes and stared at the cinder block forming the bedroom wall. It was an ugly green color – the color of hospital walls. Ugh. I was hungry. I was exhausted. I hurt. If I had been with a client, and they'd described to me the same thing I was feeling, I'd ask directly, "If your tooth could talk, what would it say?"

The answer came swiftly into my mind: "The dull pain is from a chronic response that flares up at tense times." Layman's terms would've been more to the point: "You're worrying."

How had I thought I could move to Hawaii without a job and no place to live? Moving to Hawaii was supposed to be an opportunity for me to move away from the field of psychotherapy and into the field of massage. I was burned out on the former and new to the latter. But previously unbeknownst to me, I needed a massage license to practice in Hawaii, something I hadn't needed in California. Half a dozen phone calls had taught me that bit of news my first few days in Hawaii. Back to square one in massage, and back into mental health to make a living.

Was I crazy to come here without a clearer plan than had been penciled on my refrigerator door back in California? Worry was gnawing away at me.

As I lay in bed, my tooth throbbing, I reviewed my decision to move with Laurelle. It'd come by way of *Intent,* as clear to me at that moment as it had been when it'd first occurred. Intent is the clarity that comes with direct knowledge from the Universe; it has little to do with information or decision-making, and it has nothing to do with the mind. That clarity, however, had a way of becoming blurred with the sheer stress of constant action, like a slug starting a journey across an asphalt street. I wanted to call out to the slug, "You sure you're gonna make it, buddy?"

The previous January, I'd walked down the hallway and seen Laurelle standing in front of the bathroom mirror putting on her makeup. She'd been accepted into the University of Hawaii at Manoa, and she began talking about her move to Hawaii in the fall. What would it be like to move to Hawaii? Would she continue to swim competitively? Would her major remain the same as it'd been at junior college? What would happen with her relationship with Terry?

Suddenly, without any forethought whatsoever, I'd asked, "Hey, can I move to Hawaii with you?" From reading Toltec literature, I knew that a Nagual practiced there, and I was interested in the Toltec tradition since it was a route to gain the freedom I desired. Being able to approach daily life free from preconceived ideas, values, beliefs, and emotions was the non-duality I longed for. Would moving to Hawaii be an opportunity to study with someone who claimed to walk that path? Not for an instant before that moment had I considered moving to Hawaii. It had been a moment driven by Intent, driven by a life force that didn't require a decision-making process, driven by a desire to live as each moment dictated without any deliberation.

Laurelle's eyes had opened like saucers as she exclaimed, "Oh! I'd love if you moved with me!" Her conviction was pure of heart, and in that certainty she confirmed the Intent of the moment.

And so our westward journey had begun, the journey of letting go of old structures and beliefs, of surrendering to new ones, and of Death Itself – none of which we were aware of at the moment.

Back in the present, the pain in my tooth was easing up. A vision of Bruce floated through my inner landscape, the massage therapist I'd worked with throughout my massage school training for the past three years. He was leaning over me on the massage table. His hands had stopped moving for a moment, and I'd heard him say with utter conviction, "The body doesn't lie. We can tell ourselves anything we want about what is going on, but the truth is in the body. What is your body telling you, Jessica?"

As tears sunk into the pillow, I whispered back as though he were leaning over me in my smelly, stuffy room at YMCA, "I'm worried, Bruce. I'm second-guessing myself. Maybe my reason for coming was all a huge mistake."

You took a huge risk by moving here, girl, I thought to myself, *and you have no guarantee that the Nagual will even see you.*

October 18

Bless Roy, the real estate agent! He'd looked at the rental application, saw my previous employment listings, and said, "How about trying the Hawaii State Department of Health? They're hiring. Lots of social workers have retired in the past year or so. Go to the state, they'll give you a job." He hadn't said a word about my current unemployment.

We were in! I signed a year's lease for a two-bedroom within several miles of the college. Our belongings arrived within three weeks of moving in. In the meantime, while waiting for our Matson shipping crate to arrive, we'd slept on cheap, three-inch thick pool floats placed on the linoleum floor – better than sleeping on the hard floor, but not in any way conducive to a comfortable night's sleep.

The crate contained one king-size frame and mattress, one massage table, and seventeen boxes of household and personal things. Laurelle and I had decided that I would take the bed and she would sleep on the massage table. I pushed my hands into the mattress. The resistance from the coiled springs underneath felt perfect. I couldn't wait to sleep through the whole night on my own bed rather than on beach floats taped together with duct tape. Meanwhile, ten boxes of books on shamanism and Toltec teachings had already arrived, during Laurelle's month-long stay at the YMCA. They'd been my teacher thus far on my journey. Reading those books had convinced me that seeking out a Nagual as a teacher was to be the next step on my Toltec journey.

That morning I had awakened for a second time since coming to Hawaii with an ache in my tooth that wouldn't let up. I reached up and touched my cheek. It was warm, warmer than normal. The dull throb was back. Hadn't I successfully healed the tooth a month ago while staying at the YMCA? The pain in the tooth had been absent for weeks, and I'd thought the healing had been complete.

Once again I went over the sequence of events that had led to the healing during those first few days of my arrival in Hawaii. If I returned to that moment when clarity brought conviction, that moment when Intent prompts an action regardless of a decision-making process, then perhaps I could better weather this new uncertainty.

The intense pain in the tooth just a month ago had brought with it a sense of clarity. That's what pain does; it brings with it choices we hadn't thought about without the pain itself being present. In a moment of clarity, I had known that I could heal myself. It had been a moment of Intent when I came to know that human beings have the ability to be natural healers. Recalling the story might help get my mind off the painful tooth now and onto what I might actually be able to do about the tooth. I reflected back to that moment in time on Bruce's massage table, where I'd had the experience of "no thought."

While lying on the massage table a year previous, I had drifted into a state of euphoria. It had been a natural high, like a "runner's high," and the mind had receded until there was no thought process. The last time I'd experienced "no thought" had been during an Ayahuasca journey a year previous. The experience of "no thought" is readily experienced while using plant medicines such as Ayahuasca. The two experiences, the manner in which Bruce practiced massage, called qigong bodywork, and plant medicines, were similar because participants found themselves in a black void with no time, space, or images, along with no thought process. This was the mysterious space and location for pursuing freedom outside of the many beliefs and emotions we experience on a daily basis. After going to this void, I could better recognize how my own beliefs, values, and emotions weighed me down rather than freed me up.

During that massage, the conversation between Bruce and I had stood out in my mind, but not in the manner that words are normally perceived. Spatially the words were a great distance away from my mind, not inside the mind where they usually dwelled. I usually perceived my words as a part of who I was. In recalling our words, each one appeared in the void and was connected with the word following it as though each word was a railway car linked with another railway car all arranged on a single track. Each car was linked together in a rational manner that gave meaning to the entire train. Every word was loaded with meaning, and the meaning was the weight and volume of each car on the track. Okay, so far so good – grade school grammar.

As I looked at the words, I could feel their individual and collective weight. Wordy! Heavy! Cumbersome! I saw that the words blocked the connection between Bruce and I, and were absolutely unnecessary to our exchange.

Then, as though I could see through the physicality of the words, I realized that the words carried meaning only because human beings added meaning to them! Without meaning, they were empty and useless. Now I was in graduate school with the goal of gaining a philosophy degree.

I looked at "meaning" in a concrete rather than abstract fashion, and realized that meaning held no value whatsoever beyond what we gave to it. Tears swelled under my closed eyelids as I lay face down on the massage table and I groaned. Because I was in this spatial void, I lost the sense of lying on a massage table, until I felt the warm tears squeeze from under my eyelids and drop to the floor.

The meaning we gave to things, so vitally important to us as human beings, was a peculiar human effort to define our world. All psychologically-minded human beings strived to attribute clear meaning to feelings, behaviors, and whatever events were occurring around them. Yet definition, by its nature, was limiting; and once limited, meaning then became a medium of exchange, easily convoluted, manipulated, and oftentimes misunderstood.

There was no meaning to anything! I was seated under the Bodhi tree with The Buddha.

At the same time as being in this spatial void, I began to feel Bruce's hands as he applied pressure to my skin and glided his hands along my back. The small massage room was as warm as an oven even though my realizations were light years away in black space. The realizations in that void continued.

"Meaning," while assigning high value, had no inherent value. The terrible recognition that "meaning" was without meaning, and was overloaded with expectation, led me to realize that any meaning I placed upon words, feelings, or experiences could be altered.

Aha! Meaning was malleable. Including the meaning of healing. I was the creator of my own healing, regardless of what Western medicine, or Eastern medicine for that matter, might indicate. The Intent of that moment, lying on the massage table, was crystal clear: as a human being I had innate healing abilities.

As I brought this memory into the present moment in Hawaii, I was reminded once again of the effort to heal my tooth. I put my full focus on the healing for five consecutive days during my stay at the YMCA the previous month. I was determined to bring the realization of my healing abilities during my massage with Bruce to the issue of my painful tooth. There was no "prescription" for the healing per se, but those five days were composed of meditating, visualizing, and communicating with the tooth. Sounds weird, I know, but it made perfect sense to include the tooth in its own healing, and to do that I spoke with it, enlisting it to help me in the healing process. Five days and five meditations later the pain was gone. When I was able to eat on both sides of my mouth without any pain whatsoever, I considered the healing to be complete.

Now a month later, the pain was back. While lying in bed, I reached over the side of the bed and grabbed my headphones lying on the floor. Time to listen to my special CD. My Intent was to get back to that moment of recognition that human beings are natural healers. If I could return to that moment, maybe I would know what to do next because the pain in the tooth I thought I'd healed a month ago was back with me. The CD incorporated binaural beats in the background, with soothing music as an overlay. Designed with different beats in each ear, the discordant beats cause the brain to automatically adjust to a single beat. As an outcome of that process, the brain shifts into a meditative state.

I glanced at the clock. Good! Just enough time to listen to the tape before Laurelle got home from school.

In the meditation, I lay perfectly prone with my arms at my sides. A slow paralysis took over my body. The physical mass of my body gained weight as the energetic part of me came into greater awareness. This energy body, or etheric body, was new to me. The heaviness in the physical body signaled that I was perceiving, or paying attention to, what was available outside of the awareness of my physical mass. At other times, I have continued to feel my body as it lay on the bed, but this time I was free of any bodily constraints. The chatter inside my head was minimal. For a moment there was nothing. Absolutely nada. The stillness was peaceful and deeply black. It was the void once again, and with it a blank screen.

Suddenly, veering off the screen on the left side is a dream I'd had three years ago. The dream appears as though it is a bundle of images that careen off the edge of the blank screen. I recognize the dream instantly, although it doesn't replay itself. It's like a stack of photos piled in one spot. Quickly I snatch the bundle or else it will disappear from sight, and the screen will go blank once more. This has happened before. I have "defined" the experience as one of being in the void with no mind, and knowledge approaches without so much as a knock on the door. Suddenly, and inexplicably, it is there.

Many people would say that the purpose of meditation is to

keep that screen blank, or to simply watch what floats by. Whatever floats across that screen can keep right on floating until it exits the screen. I'd done that. But I also sometimes grabbed onto images that almost got away. The near escape of those images would grab my attention.

"Wait! What is that?" My awareness hooks into the fleeting imagery of the past dream. I reach out and pull it back. The action sequence occurs in a millisecond, so fast that often the image is long gone before I am able to retrieve it. That's okay with me. I figure the images I miss aren't ready for exposure, and the images I catch are ripe for expression.

The dream had originally occurred while I'd been in Montana for a week-long workshop with a shaman from California, Carol Proudfoot-Edgar. The shaman had asked four volunteers to dream that evening, one for each of the four directions. I had volunteered for the South. Looking back, I can't say why I had volunteered; I was shy and quiet, and reporting a dream to twenty women in addition to having the dream in the first place was something I'd never done before. Nerves had almost gotten the best of me. Could I dream on demand? But the dream had shown up very early the next morning before the mist had rolled through the freshly mown field of hay outside my bedroom window, and the sun was still lying asleep behind the Rocky Mountains.

Three images had appeared. One was the chest of a huge bear, bearing the claw marks of another of its kind with bright red blood flowing. The second image was of scat lying on forest pine needles intermingled with deep, wine-red berries. The third image was of a broad river flowing gently, a Mississippi of red liquid.

Suddenly I hear the words, "... your past, present, and future. Step into the future. It is movement, flow, power."

The announcement was over. So was the meditation and it had had nothing to do with the healing of my tooth. Odd as it may sound, I was familiar with hearing a voice while in a meditative state. I believed the voice to be my higher self or higher consciousness. Toltec teachings would say that voice comes from the etheric or energy body that is developed during dreaming practices.

Odder still, even though I accepted the voice, which had been developed through dreaming as my own, I was hoping the Nagual in Hawaii would clarify how higher consciousness could be further developed. Many experiences aren't easily put into words, and I wanted input from her as the Nagual, or the expert in shamanistic and Toltec practices, to clarify for me what to do when I didn't understand what the voice indicated for me to do.

Slowly, I moved my limbs as my body awakened. I hadn't felt the tooth throbbing once throughout the entire meditation. My body really had been in a state of paralysis, but the pain was back in full force now. With it came the question I'd been asking myself all month: When was I going to contact the Nagual? Maybe she could help with the healing of my tooth. Maybe she could clarify for me what was happening during so many of my meditative experiences. At the moment, despite previous experiences of certainty, I didn't know how to put into practice what I knew I was capable of as a healer. I felt like the slug that was halfway across the warm asphalt, unsure as to whether or not I'd make it all the way across.

October 22

"So do you want the job, or not?" The woman seated across the desk looked at me with tired eyes and a wan smile. My eyes kept dropping to the scar that ran down her neck onto the center of her chest like a swollen blood vessel lying on top of her skin rather than underneath. Absurdly, I wondered why she was wearing such a low-necked blouse. I got the impression she had interviewed one too many people that week and just wanted to fill the position as soon as possible. It was my second interview, and I expected the offer. However, between interview one and interview two another agency had called.

I had a second interview with agency two scheduled for that afternoon. The first position was program director of a residential treatment home for adolescent girls (the position with the worn-out administrator). The second position was clinical therapist with adolescents at a foster agency. I needed another day to make the decision.

"Can I get back with you on my answer tomorrow?" I asked. We both knew that was code in the human services field for "I'm weighing my options," but the offer was on the table and she wouldn't retract it at that point. I had the time I needed to determine which job would be the best fit, not only for me but for the agencies, too. I stood up and extended my hand. She shoved my resume into a folder on her desk before taking my hand in return.

"I'll be in touch," I said.

"Call HR (Human Resources) if you're interested," she replied tiredly. "I'll be out of the office tomorrow."

I drove the speed limit on the freeway (it was done that way there – quite a shock from being a lead-foot California driver!), pondering both jobs. I'd been in Hawaii for a month, and based on my efforts at sending out two dozen resumes and waiting for interested phone calls, I'd learned three things: Hawaii had plenty of positions open in the human service sector, few positions in massage for a masseuse without a license, and no one was in any hurry to hire.

That's why I was pleased to have two (almost) options in the offing. Based on my past experience, the program director position was a logical progression in job responsibilities. On the other hand, the program therapist position was unique because in Hawaii the position was not combined with case management, and case management had been a huge contributor to my burnout.

Returning to human services was a 180-degree turn, an about-face back into the field I'd been endeavoring to leave for two years. I was okay with it though. Life took unexpected turns, and this appeared to be one of them. I'd go with the flow, and any intended purpose would reveal itself in time. One thing I did have within my grasp was which job to accept, assuming the second agency would offer me the position. For the time being, the best position would be the one that would allow the time and energy to do what I really wanted to be doing while also paying the bills.

Let me be direct here, and hopefully I won't sound mercenary. I wanted the position that would allow me the time and energy to write on my off-hours. The reason I recognized the administrator's attitude was because it was my own. Any sense of altruism toward working in my field of expertise had gone out the window a long while ago. I was tired of working in human services and counseling. For two years I'd attended massage school in order to leave the field of working with "challenged" children. For the time being, however, the door into the massage field in Hawaii was closed. The field I had planned on moving into was no longer an option, so back I was going into human services in order to make a living. Mercenary or not, it was the truth.

November 25

I met the Nagual! I had waited a long time to speak with her. Lots of people had wanted to speak with her if numbers were any indicator. In the center of my being I knew exactly why I'd moved to Hawaii – to apprentice with this very woman – but once in Hawaii, I'd been having a difficult time contacting her. Easy enough to dream a dream, to plan out coordinates to make that dream come true, and then to wait, and then to wait some more – much more difficult to stand face to face with that same dream.

My action of severing one life to begin another wasn't about what I *believed* to be true for me; it was "right action," meaning that, regardless of my feelings or thoughts, coming to Hawaii to study with this woman had been the action called for at that very moment in time. That she might say no was not a viable option, at least while I had been on the mainland packing up. Now that I was there, I was in the right place at the right time, in a manner of speaking, but that didn't mean I wasn't going to do something stupid as a result of how nervous I felt standing within arm's reach of her. I knew myself well and didn't quite trust that "right action" would overcome my anxiety in the moment.

Her center was a converted house in town, located in a quasi-industrial area, two blocks from City Hall. I knew that piece of information because I had been at City Hall the previous week applying for my driver's license.

I walked up the outside steps to get to the second story, and upon entering the double doors I paused to look around. It was an open house and those in attendance were invited to wander through the place. A large, open living room, free of furniture, was to my right. Vendors were seated on the carpet with their wares. Along the long wall facing the street were open windows looking onto a lanai. Areca palms lined the outdoor patio and swayed with a gentle Kona breeze that cooled off the end of the eighty-degree summer heat.

Off the entryway to the left was a small altar room with a tall Kwan Yen statue, a Buddha, and tea lights placed randomly around the room. Incense burned in a brass bowl in front of Kwan Yen. The smoke reminded me of my days at the sweat lodge and smelled of sage and sweet grass. The kitchen area was at the end of the entryway, next to a door leading into a front bathroom, and beyond were three converted bedrooms – an office, a massage room, and a large square closet that was lined with mirrors but otherwise empty.

At the entrance a clipboard lay on a divide between the main living room and the entryway. Those people attending could sign up for energy work, cleansings, breath work, or Tarot readings. I was single-minded. I was there to speak with the Nagual, and anything else felt like a distraction.

What if she actually said no? Something that had seemed impossible six months ago. What if she said, "You moved here with the sole purpose of studying with me and didn't contact me before arriving? What were you thinking?" I quickly signed up to speak with the Nagual, unable to answer those questions, and then added my signature under the Tarot reading as an afterthought. A distraction at the moment would be a good thing.

"Looks like you're experiencing a block with your writing," said the woman reading the Tarot. It's the only thing I remember about the reading. A full month with no work and I had not been able to put a single word on paper. She couldn't have been more on target. Discouraged to hear my predicament read in the cards so clearly, I stood up and headed for the front door.

"I'll e-mail the Nagual," I muttered as I headed down the outside steps. I sighed, feeling deflated and dejected. Halfway down the steps, I stopped, and like an errant child being grabbed by the nape of the neck, I turned myself around and trudged back up the stairs. *Nope, you're not going to do anything stupid,* I said to myself. *You're here to meet the Nagual. That's why you moved across the Pacific Ocean. It's time to meet her.*

I walked back into the entryway and looked around. Who was she? Amusing how people we anticipate meeting look in our imaginations. There were several women I could picture as being the Nagual. One woman, in her mid-fifties with gray streaks running through her shoulder-length brown hair, wore a flowing purple skirt, a lacy white tank top, and lots of turquoise and silver jewelry. Her smile was open, her laugh infectious.

Another woman was tall and tanned, her hair cut short and severe. She held her shoulders upright. I pictured her mother, telling her at puberty, "Stop drooping. Stand up straight!" Her smile was more stern than warm. I continued to watch as people spoke with each other, wandered from room to room, and listened for their names to be called.

Finally I made the connection: Ah! There she was! She's the woman who continued to come and go from the first doorway at the end of the entryway. Of course. It's her office. I'd observed her earlier but hadn't made the connection that she was the Nagual, because my expectations were on flowing skirts and stern smiles. Mid-to-late fifties in age and shorter than I in height, the Nagual carried a bit of weight, not too much, and not too little, either. Her blond hair was cropped below the ears and curly, as women of her age tend to wear, and she had on khaki shorts and a loose, comfortable blouse.

Her eyes were her dominant feature, piercingly blue, not in color but in depth, and she placed them on people and objects with ease and precision at the same time, like a knife slicing through a block of butter. And just at the moment I identified who she was, she called my name.

I followed her into the office. She sat down, indicating for me to do the same, and handed me a small deck of cards. "Pick one," she prompted. She gazed at me intently with barely the hint of a smile on her face. Shuffling the cards, I vaguely remembered putting my signature down earlier for some sort of angel card reading. In reality, I'd signed simply because her name was at the top of the activity offered.

"I came today to ask a few questions," I said to the Nagual. I glanced down at the deck of cards. I shuffled them absent-mindedly trying to think of how to phrase my first question. What was my question? I couldn't just walk into her office and blurt out, "Can I be your apprentice?" The temperature in the office suddenly spiked dangerously high. I lost my hearing. For a moment, there was absolute stillness in the room as I grasped for my next words. The music faded and some forty people outside the office went silent. I was in a vacuum of stillness, filled with anxiety.

Nearly frantic, I shuffled the cards again and tried to organize a coherent sentence from within the walls of my paralyzed mind. I longed to say, "I moved here a month ago from the mainland in order to study with you. Are you taking apprentices?" Such a simple and direct question would have gone to the heart of the matter, but I couldn't utter a word.

It wasn't audacity that had brought me there; it was "right action." But suddenly those words sounded strange. For me, "right action" meant I was on the path that was correct for me; though suddenly being seated in front of the Nagual, with the expectation that I would become her apprentice, it sounded preposterous.

I chose a card slowly. The objects in my peripheral vision disappeared as I focused on the stack of cards on my lap. The heat from my chest threatened to burn through my shirt, and I was sure the thumping of my heart was audible. I turned the card over. It had the word "Healing" on it. Handing it to the Nagual, I sighed as though the upheaval inside had suddenly evaporated.

"That fits, because my question is about healing," I stated as though those were the words I'd meant to say all along, and the heat in the room and in my chest were merely due to the temperature of a Hawaiian summer day. I launched into the story of my tooth and my attempts at self-healing, as though that topic was the very reason I was seated in her office.

"I tried to heal my tooth several months ago but there's still a throbbing in it," I blurted out. I told the Nagual about my recent move to the island and the acquisition of a job, including the fact that health insurance was on its way. I emphasized that it was important to me to understand my attempts at self-healing before I saw a dentist. I told her that it seemed to me that human beings handed over their power to heal themselves too easily into the hands of "professional" healers. I had wanted to exercise my innate healing abilities, but somewhere along the way the healing had been incomplete.

Whew, my words all sounded like I'd fallen into a rabbit hole, and I was meandering along its alleyways without any light. I couldn't find my way out. The Nagual sat still as a statue with her eyes placed on me. She didn't seek to speak or to intervene but listened attentively as I spoke.

"I believe all of us have the capacity to be healers, but maybe there are steps to healing that I haven't tried," I faltered. Trying to counter my doubt with belief, I had concluded too easily that my healing effort had been a failure. I could hear the self-doubt in my voice.

"So I suppose that means I didn't really heal it," my voice quivered. "I thought I knew what healing was..." my voice trailing off. I was far afield of where I wanted to be for my first conversation with the Nagual. My tooth was not what I wanted to be discussing! I stopped talking. Meanwhile, the Nagual's eyes assessed the situation with my story and me at the center.

"Healing is not often about what we think it is," she slowly responded. "It is multidimensional. If the healing doesn't happen the way we think it should, it may be that it is there for another reason." The Nagual paused and looked at me. Now it was my turn to be silent. She continued, saying more about healing from a multifaceted perspective, but the words wafted out the window as though they were the Kona wind.

I'm not talking about healing as a metaphor! I screamed inside my mind. I knew the toothache was about my worry, and once I'd made that connection, the pain from the tooth had eased. At that moment it was just a low-grade throb. None of my healing efforts had been successful and I didn't know why. But I couldn't for the life of me say anything else without fear of sounding argumentative. Plunging into another question seemed to be the best means of moving the conversation away from my muddled thinking.

"I've studied Toltec ideas for several years on my own," I said. "I'm at a point where I'm not able to find answers to my questions. I hear you have classes and do private counseling." I hadn't mentioned the "a" word, but was pleased that maybe I'd been able to turn the conversation back to my reason for being seated in her office. Maybe I'd walked myself out of that rabbit hole.

The Nagual responded by telling me about her new plans for the upcoming year, about the regular classes she conducted on Tuesday and Thursday evenings, and about the workshops she offered intermittently through the year. With a casualness I was certainly not feeling on my side of the desk, the Nagual asked, "Would you like to come to one of the midweek classes?"

"Yes." I nodded my head. I dared not say more, apart from asking the day and time of the class. The fiasco brought on by my first question loomed too dangerously near at hand. The Nagual was neither with nor without a smile, although her eyes were clear and calm. I felt a moment of stillness, and the blush threatening to creep up my neck subsided after she invited me to attend her class. I stood and shook the Nagual's hand, thanking her for the reading. Maybe the multidirectional aspect of my healing would become evident to me, and I would understand what had happened with my tooth. Right then, however, I just wanted to bolt out of the office.

Walking directly to the front door, I left the gathering without saying a word to anyone else. I pulled my car door open and slumped into the driver's seat one second before tears burst from my eyes. Turning on the ignition, I put the car into reverse and backed up. Tears flooded my view but I didn't care. The tears were coming as quick as a flash flood overflows the banks of a dry desert gorge. Strangely, the wetness from the tears felt comforting. Not a good idea to be driving in traffic, but I had to get away. The tears released from a place I hadn't even known they occupied. I pulled over to the side of the road, out of eyesight of the Nagual's place. Sobbing, I leaned over the steering wheel.

My thoughts tumbled out as quickly as the tears fell. My feelings overwhelmed me as though a dam had been released. The events leading to this moment felt like a twenty-foot wall of water that I'd tried to outrun for too long.

Six months ago I'd known with certainty that it was time to study with a Nagual. All of my experiences up to that point had come from one of two sources: books or self-taught, both solitary endeavors. Time to put myself under the tutelage of someone known for being an expert in the field.

I longed for someone to define for me how to conduct healing, how to develop my dreaming abilities further, how to access states of mind and states of being outside daily reality because I believed those practices would lead me to a state of freedom. Most importantly, a Nagual, a teacher in the Toltec tradition, would teach me how to gain a state of non-duality.

Until that moment, I hadn't realized how alone I'd been in studying the Toltec path. The relief was overwhelming that I'd finally made it to the doorstep of a Nagual, someone who knew the knowledge and experience of having gained personal freedom for herself. And despite my not being able to express myself clearly, she'd invited me back.

December 3

Curious to see what would take place during the Nagual's evening meetings, I'd arrived early. This was my first evening meeting with the Nagual since our introduction during the previous week at the Center's open house. Finally, I was seated with a Nagual teacher! What did she do during the meetings? What did the apprentices do? What happened each evening? When I arrived, six or eight women had been seated in a circle on the carpet in the large meeting room. Several of them I recognized from the week before. Based on our mutual nods and smiles, they also recognized me. I sat down.

After greeting everyone seated cross-legged on the carpet, the Nagual began to speak. Her lecture for the evening was about the connecting link of love that unites all human beings regardless of the path they'd chosen to follow.

"Love transcends even the Toltec path because it is a greater, more encompassing force than any singular path," the Nagual said. "Love makes the world go round, and even though that's a cliché, it is indeed how things operate."

"Love has different meanings, doesn't it?" asked a woman. "Because I've been married for thirty-seven years and I wouldn't say my love for my husband is what makes the world go round." She had a mischievous grin on her face. She had strawberry blond hair in a bob cut, a button nose covered with freckles, and pale blue eyes. Another woman snickered at her comment.

The Nagual didn't acknowledge the woman's sarcasm directly but responded with her next comment.

"I'm not talking about love for others," the Nagual countered. "Love for others is important but it starts with the love you have for yourself. Without love for yourself, your ability to love others will soon run dry."

"What about service to others?" Another woman spoke up. "I

know Carol is being silly but I'm with her: what kind of love are you talking about? As a social worker, I feel the work I do with the homeless is all about love."

The Nagual didn't respond directly to this speaker either but paused for a moment as if to consider a change in the direction of her lecture.

"There was a time in my life when I had no love for myself, but I wasn't aware of that fact. All I knew was that my life had no meaning. I'd lost two successful businesses, and lost my mother in a car accident that looked suspiciously like a suicide. Nothing made sense to me. The last thing I would have acknowledged at that time was that I had no love for myself. It wasn't in the equation until the only solution I could arrive at was to take my own life, too. I felt like a failure."

It wasn't the first time the circle of women had heard this story, I was certain. Discussion stopped as the Nagual told the story of awakening from her failed suicide and feeling disgust at the foiled attempt. From the bottom of that pit of despair, she rose, made a physical move across country to start a new life, and eventually found the Nagual who would become her own teacher.

Her talk of love triggered my own painful memories, even though I suspected she meant her story to be hopeful. For a moment, I had a feeling of déjà vu: I was seated in a church pew, listening to a testimonial. My understanding of "love" was rooted in the church and in a religion in which love was a payoff for acknowledging that I was inadequate in this lifetime unless I accepted Jesus as Savior. I also understood the psychological concepts of self-worth and self-acceptance; what I was missing was an understanding of how self-worth and self-love were the driving forces on the Toltec path. And I still didn't understand how love for myself would lead me to freedom. I raised my hand.

"Three years ago, spirit could never have spoken to me

through the words you're using," I said. "I was fresh out of a twenty-year marriage to a pastor and 'love' had too many painful connotations. Love was about obeying the commands of a God who called me a sinner. I don't see the connection. How does love drive a person on the Toltec path?"

"To begin with," the Nagual responded, "love is inclusive of every path out there. Everything we do and everything we are is generated from a wellspring of love. But if we don't get to the place of love for ourselves and for others, we're simply rearranging deck chairs on the Titanic, making things important that are not lasting." The metaphor was an intriguing one, but I still failed to grasp how love was the answer.

My hand shot up again. "If the journey is really about love, I feel tricked. Before coming here, my reading and experiences on the Toltec path came primarily from Carlos Castaneda, and he doesn't mention love."

"Everyone experiences the path differently, not right, not wrong, but different," the Nagual said curtly. Her tone of voice said there wasn't going to be any more discussion.

Without knowing why, I felt chastised. Suddenly I noticed that no one else had spoken during our exchange. Had I breached a social norm in the group without knowing it? I sat silent. The Nagual spoke further.

"Our connecting link with Spirit is evidenced by love. Without love, there is no connection to Spirit. The two are synonymous."

I had trouble listening from then on. My connecting link with Castaneda had been just what I'd needed, at a time I needed it most, and yet he never mentioned love. He was adamant on taking action though. Action was imperative in our lives if we expected to get beyond our own self-concepts. Action was what had brought me to Hawaii. Yes, Castaneda asked lots of questions that were off course, he was contrary at every turn, and he was a bona fide drama queen. Many of his actions ran counter to acting from a stance of love, yet I'd started my journey with his experiences as my guide. To hear the Nagual's stance on love as it connected with the Toltec path was disconcerting to me.

I observed the group as they responded to the Nagual, listening carefully to their questions and comments. Their words were not laced with terminology from other writers on the Toltec path. I'd read all of the Toltec writers I knew to read. I'd read them and then read them again. At the end of the day, I'd always found myself with Carlos Castaneda in hand.

Tonight my devotion, my adoration, and my immersion into Castaneda's language ran headlong into the Nagual's words, as though they were two football teams in a scrimmage, charging each other and dog piling, helmets clashing, cleats digging, clods of grass flying. Never had I been so aware of my attachment to language. From the many things the Nagual shared during her lecture, I was hung up on her use of the word "love" and its totality for her on the Toltec path. At the end of her lecture, the Nagual asked if there were any questions.

"Your experience of the Toltec path is very different from mine," I said soberly. It was an invitation for more discussion but there wasn't going to be any further conversation. The Nagual said no more on the subject.

"It's time for the evening meditation," she announced, then. She walked to her office and returned with a large ceramic singing bowl. Everyone in the group began to push aside their belongings and lie down on the carpet. The Nagual directed everyone to position their feet in the center of the circle with their heads facing the perimeter, as though we were spokes on a wheel. She began to play the singing bowl by circling the mallet in her hand around the rim of the bowl, creating a lyrical sound.

I was familiar with going on meditative journeys via sound. I looked forward to the journey, even though at the moment I was feeling the loss of familiar words and the strangeness of new words to describe the journey I believed myself to be on. The sound of the bowl transported me into a meditative state immediately.

A few minutes into the evening's meditation, with my eyes closed and a black screen before me, a crow flew into the open window. Landing on the carpet, the crow hip-hopped over to me. I was thrilled to see Crow! The last time Crow had shown up had been six months prior in California. Anyone living in California wouldn't think much of that statement. There were a million crows living in California, and a crow sighting wasn't unusual, but that one had been auspicious. I'd been returning to the condo complex after an early morning run, and when I'd entered the walk-in gate on the northeast corner of the complex, above my head seated on the telephone wires, a crow had begun to caw. Again, not too unusual. The moment it became unusual was when the crow flew directly over my head as I walked toward three buildings with an open space between them. I stood at the juncture where the ends of the three buildings nearly conjoined in a space perhaps twenty-by-twenty feet. From the sidewalk, with foliage on both sides and open sky above me, I noticed nothing that would ostensibly draw Crow to that location apart from his attention placed on me. Crow began cawing, rasping, and clicking – crow language heard by millions of southern Californians.

Standing there, gazing at the crow not one story above me, an even odder thing occurred: four more crows joined us. In the space of less than one minute, five crows were dipping, diving, and flying in tight circles in the air directly above, yelping, yipping, and chattering away. Yep, crows were auspicious for me! Crows flying into a room weren't happenstance, I knew that much.

Back in the meditation room, Crow's presence announced to me: "This is a good place for you to be. Stay awhile." No other form of agreement could have been a stronger omen. During the Nagual's talk, a burden had been brewing inside me. Crow's message was in direct response to my turmoil. My turmoil was in hearing the Nagual's emphasis on love as a foundation of walking the path. I'd never considered that love was a binding, driving force on the Toltec path. Where were the concepts I was familiar with? intent, dreaming and tracking, heightened awareness, and the assemblage point – all terms familiar to the Toltec path I knew.

To compound my agitation an old saying flashed through my mind the moment Crow's message came to an end: "A blackbird flying into a room signifies death."

"Whose death?" I shot at Crow just as he lifted his jet-black wings and veered for the open window. "Whose death?" I insisted. He gave no answer.

The meditation ended and everyone eased his or her body into a seated position in the circle. The Nagual did a check in. "Anyone want to share what happened for you during the meditation?"

I spoke immediately. "A crow flew into the window during my meditation. A blackbird flying into a room is an omen of death." I choked on the last word, a few hot tears dropping from the corner of my eyes. Death was a word as loaded with meaning as love, and at the moment, I didn't have a clear understanding of either. I paused for an instant, blinking to ease the tears.

"All evening I've been trying to translate from one language to another," I said. "It's been slow going."

"Those are just words," replied the Nagual. "Your confusion with words is not about the difficulty in learning a new language. It's in adjusting to a different energy level. You are opening yourself to a new experience, and words become an easy shield for you to defend against the experience."

If I knew then what I know now, I would have known that my position in the West of the medicine wheel was already challenging me with Death. The death of a language I was comfortable and familiar with was at my doorstep, and the death of my ideas and values around money was just around the corner. On that evening, I didn't know that Death was actively pursuing me through these two arenas, and like the moth that hovers too near a light bulb, I was courting a similar demise.

December 13

"It's time to get back to mirror meditations tonight," the Nagual announced.

Mirror meditation was new to me. The only time I'd done a mirror meditation was the time I'd put on a lion mask. That experience had turned out oddly, to say the least, so I was curious about doing a meditation in the Nagual's mirrored closet. The Nagual began the evening with a lecture on the purpose for doing mirror meditations. She shared that her apprenticeship experience of doing mirror meditations had brought on abject terror and fear for her. The purpose for the mirror in the meditation was as a reflection of our internal state of being. The meditation via the mirror exposed our inner beings and was the vehicle for us to clear the fears, imbalance, and dis-ease each one of us harbored. She emphasized the word "disease" with a hyphen to accentuate the meaning as disequilibrium rather than medical pathology.

The memory of my first experience with a mirror meditation came back to me while seated with the other women in a circle on the carpet. At the time, I had constructed the lion mask by following directions from a book I was reading. The facial structure of the mask was constructed from an old metal clothes hanger and then covered with plaster strips to fill in the facial features. I had painted the mask and included cloth strips for the lion's mane.

Seating myself in front of my bathroom vanity, I had lit a candle and positioned it to the left of my face. Then I'd put the mask on. It had been late at night, no sound of traffic from the street outside. I had been home alone. The night had been quiet enough to hear the flame from the candle flicker and begin to lick at the small pool of melted wax in its center.

Immediately upon donning the mask, my awareness had

shifted. Castaneda would've said I'd gone into heightened awareness, or the experience of moving away from the perception of my immediate surroundings, either internally or externally or both. There had been a mild shift of the assemblage point, the perception I was most familiar with, causing my perception to move away from its normal position of how I viewed the world on a daily basis. I was no longer seated before a mirror with a lion mask covering my face. The assemblage point had moved from its familiar position, and that movement had brought with it a change in my point of view and how I felt. The view of what I was facing was literally not what it had been a moment before. The lion had shifted from the physical realm to the spiritual realm. A shift like this could be pleasant and agreeable, or awkward and discomfiting, even jolting; however, I hadn't known that putting a mask on could be so creepy.

On that night, spooky, oppressive feelings had erupted as I watched the mask in the mirror. I was no longer the "me" that I was consciously aware of. I had watched as the lion's head morphed and became another me in the eerie glow of the candle-light. Sitting perfectly still, I had waited while the spookiness filled me. After at most maybe fifteen minutes, I had ripped off the mask, blown out the candle, and dived into bed. That had been my one and only mirror meditation. The perceptual shift had been unfamiliar to me, and I had bolted out of the experience to return to a familiar state. Now the Nagual was saying that those fearful feelings were an expression of my inner being.

After the Nagual's lecture, I better understood why my experience with the lion mask had thrown me into such turmoil a year ago. The purpose of the mirror meditations was to draw out those aspects of ourselves that needed clearing out. When we're carrying internal heaviness in the form of memories and experiences that don't support well-being and non-duality, those psychic experiences cause weightiness within our being. Unless those experiences are cleared from our psyches, our hearts, and our minds, we feel cluttered and lack clarity in our lives. However, I didn't know all this during my first mirror meditation.

"Oh no!" Carol groaned as the Nagual stated the Intent for the remainder of the evening, "Not another mirror meditation!" But she rescinded her statement when others began to tease her. The Nagual looked at her as though to say, "Yep, that's what I mean." Aloud she said, "It's time to start doing them again. There are some things that need to be cleaned out around here."

Sounds like a backstory there, I thought, as I looked around to see others' reactions. No one commented and we all rose from the carpet to head for the back room with the mirrored closet.

I sat cross-legged with my back straight. Three other people were seated behind me, each of us the corner of a square, all with our backs to each other and the front of our bodies facing the closet walls. Large mirrors covered the walls of the six-by-six-foot closet. The room was dark except for a single tea candle placed in the center of the carpeted floor. The candle burned valiantly against the shadowy interior. The mirrors multiplied its light geometrically on each of the four walls. I gazed at my reflection in the mirror and closed my eyes halfway, softening the gaze. The women around me settled in, and I did the same.

The power of the mirror meditation began to influence my inner vision. By the stillness in the small closet, I suspected the three women seated around me were also moving into their own inner journey. Slowly, my peripheral view began to expand at the same time the ceiling began to lower. I found myself seated on a large portico, a freestanding building not attached to any other structure. Surrounding me were women seated before small individual braziers, crackling warmly at each woman's crossed feet. Like me, the women were quiet and meditative. The feeling was one of solitude amongst collective unity, as though the uniqueness of each woman could be felt even though we all looked alike. I knew each woman, and each was doing the very same thing that I was doing. Our occupation was to sit before these fires, to keep them tended and burning. Our devotion was placed as an offering into the flames crackling before us. The portico was filled with an aroma of contemplation and reverence.

All of the women wore robes and burkas. Our mouths were uncovered but no one spoke. I turned slightly to my right and noticed a woman wearing a cream robe and matching burka. She was a member of the women's council. With a gasp, I recognized the woman: it was me! My mouth opened and then closed again without uttering a sound. My body was outside of myself, as though I was observing an unfamiliar being. That being was contemplative with nowhere else that she needed to be, only to be seated and tending her fire.

I waited for the woman seated before me to utter a word or to make a gesture, but she sat in complete stillness. The peace was pervasive. Like a pond without a ripple, nothing moved from either above or below the surface to break the mirror-like smoothness of the water. No jolt, no creepy feeling. As a member of the group, I belonged there. Satisfaction filled me, and I sat in the sweet stillness until the Nagual called all of us back from the meditation.

Seated outside the mirrored closet for twenty minutes while others were inside for their meditation, I reflected on my experience. What a difference the experience had been from my first lion meditation! Relief flooded me. The satisfaction of being seated in silence before a small fire felt much like easing into a favorite yoga position, peaceful and still. The awareness that I was at the right place at the right time permeated my being just as the smoke from the brazier had permeated the air around me while meditating.

The Nagual closed the evening by giving us surprise homework. "From now on, I want you to do mirror meditations nightly at home. Light a candle and set it behind a clear glass of water. Look into the mirror for as long as you can. When the meditation is over, take the glass of water and pour it either down a drain or into the earth. Don't drink the water as it has become the container for your experience and you don't want to re-ingest it." Then she cackled as though she were a witch standing over a caldron stirring a witchy brew as all of us gathered our things to go home.

December 19

Money is a tricky thing to negotiate when there's no tangible price tag. In our initial conversation, the Nagual informed me that she charged her students a monthly fee. "Nowadays, it is expected that students contribute to the teachings they receive," she'd stated. The idea of paying for weekly teachings didn't sit well with me, but I had no argument with which to refute it. Simply saying I had no idea what to contribute was not likely to make matters change. Naïveté is never a strong debate point. Besides, I knew I was meant to be studying with the Nagual. I knew it long before I'd ever gotten on the plane to come to Hawaii. Money wasn't going to be the deal breaker, but without a doubt, it was going to factor into our relationship. That's the inherent nature of any kind of monetary exchange.

I understood "fair exchange" in a market society. Anyone devoting their time to the instruction of students or clients or customers needed to be reimbursed at a fair price. I had made a living providing psychotherapy to clients who paid me well for that service. As the wife of a minister, we had tithed ten percent of our income to the Church for many years. The act of paying for services wasn't an issue. What was an issue was how to determine fair exchange.

The philosophical dilemma, or "tension" would be a better term, of a teacher and student relationship founded in monetary exchange intrigued me. One psychotherapy client would pay me $40 for a session and another would pay me $100. Did my services change? Nope. Castaneda took bags of groceries to Don Juan. Fair exchange for a ten-year apprenticeship? Hardly. Don Juan hadn't needed material or monetary donations from Castaneda; he had been financially stable although he presented himself as an older gentleman living in a frugal hut in the Sonoran Desert. Circumstances are different nowadays and apprenticeships have become a business, yet I have never read about fees charged by Naguals.

In all of my readings involving apprenticeships, an exchange of money had scarcely been mentioned. The emphasis had been placed on the spiritual or the synchronistic point of contact between the Nagual and the apprentice. So-and-so happened to be in an unusual place at an unusual time and the Nagual appeared, signaling the beginning of an apprenticeship. Or, the Nagual waited for spirit to point out the apprentice with an omen. From then on, the stories that involved the journey or the quest had been highlighted, and the basic exchange rate that sustained the journey had been glossed over.

Was the exchange of money not kosher to discuss in the stories of Naguals and apprentices? Eventually, the topic would come up between the Nagual and I, but meanwhile, I couldn't see how my budget could support one more financial commitment. We were already eating twenty-six-cent noodle packets by the end of the week. On the other hand, I had a sense of certainty that we would be able to come to an agreement about payment for her services.

I wasn't the only student to question the issue of payment for services. Other students had approached her long before my arrival. One evening I was within earshot of a discussion about payment to the Nagual, and it wasn't about money per se, but barter. The eavesdropping was unintentional, although it provided me with a possible solution to my dilemma, which came in an unexpected manner

"Did you know that she cleans the Nagual's house for payment toward classes?" I overheard one student saying to another. "Yeah, I heard that too, and Barb watches her animals when she travels," said the other. Seemed the Nagual bartered for services in exchange for attendance at class. My solution arrived on the heels of the next comment: "... and Karen used to give her massages, but she's no longer coming to class." My bartering power immediately became apparent!

I approached the Nagual and offered my barter. She agreed to a massage a week in exchange for attendance at one weekly class. I was elated! I suggested an initial massage in order for her to experience my massage style.

Massage is a funny business, as is psychotherapy. There is no shortage of style and interpretation in the practice of these two arts. In addition to my formal massage training, I had trained with Bruce, whose giftedness lay in being able to energetically read a body with his hands. If he could have been a student of Wilhelm Reich, I'm sure he would have been. He could read the psychological and physiological health of a body via his massage. That, combined with years of solid massage work at the office of a chiropractor, made Bruce simply the best massage therapist around. Mentoring me during the years I attended massage school, he taught me what those who practice energy work in conjunction with massage know, which is this one essential truth: the body doesn't lie. The body is a portal into a person's well-being.

I wanted the Nagual to know of my sincere interest in my massage practice. I wanted her to be comfortable with what I had to offer, because once I began doing consistent massage work on her, I would be able to "read" her body just as Bruce had taught me to do. Bodywork is an intimate exchange, and I wanted the Nagual to be fully aware of the agreement she was making with me. There was no doubt in my mind the Nagual had already read my energy (because that's what Naguals do), and our barter arrangement would now allow me to give her something in exchange.

December 29

The morning was early. The light coming through the window fell on my legs like syrup being poured over a warm pancake. The dream lingered. A grin broke over my face even though no one was witness to it. This was the first dream in which the Nagual had joined me since my move to Hawaii. I'd been waiting for her to show up!

My experience in practicing Toltec concepts of dreaming factored into my excitement. When a Nagual enters a student's dreams, it signals that a working alliance has been formed between the Nagual and the student. It also signals that dreaming practices have evolved sufficiently for both the Nagual and student for the dreaming to occur in the first place.

In the dream, I look across a large green expanse and see energy superimposed onto the scene, shimmering bubbles of effervescence that blanket the lawn. Hundreds of lines converge to form a filigreed veil. A door in the energy lines appears and then instantly disappears, as though the door were playing hide and seek. My head turns. A car is parked to my left that I hadn't noticed a moment before. The lines blanketing the car are delicate strings of light, pulsing and throbbing, streams of energy curious and conscious of their own awareness. They add magic to what is otherwise an ordinary scene.

"I can see the energy lines!" I cry, turning to the Nagual, who is seated alongside me in the dream. I surmise that she has just walked in through the door, since she wasn't there a moment ago. She is dressed in a beaded outfit that shimmers much like the energy popping and sparkling around us. *This is what electricity looks like,* I realize. The Nagual's next movements startle me. Her body begins to shimmy like the lines dancing around her. She flails her arms and legs in all directions as though she's just been plugged into a socket. "I knew it!" she cries. "I knew you could see them!" I awoke feeling a connection to the Nagual that I hadn't felt before having the dream as though there was budding camaraderie between us.

In the short time I'd been with the Nagual, I'd noticed that she didn't compliment or hand out "attaboys" often. She wasn't one to use verbal encouragement as a teaching tool, so her action in my dream was unexpected. More often than not, she would use reprimand for direction to individual students. "We've talked about this before; I see you're doing it again" would more likely come from her mouth than an inquisitive prompt or gentle directive. She didn't pull any punches or soft peddle. Some might call it "tough love." For her to show excitement was unexpected and an encouragement regarding my dreaming abilities.

Savoring the dream, I lay still for a few more minutes. Later that morning I was scheduled to go to the Center for a once-a-month house cleaning. I wondered whether I would tell the Nagual about the dream or whether she already knew where she had been the previous night in the dreamtime? My expectation was that she would know where she'd traveled while dreaming and to whom she'd made a visit.

I arrived at the Center that morning to see four or five other women, some of whom I remembered meeting the first evening I'd attended. Immediately, several women begin to question the Nagual about their dreaming from the previous night.

They accused her in friendly tones: "What were you doing last night? You were out and about, weren't you?" It sounded as though the Nagual met with these women at different times, because I didn't recognize all of them from the Tuesday meetings. I looked from the Nagual to the women and then back again, waiting to see who would speak next.

"I instructed the apprentices to look for me in their dreams last night," said the Nagual as she turned to me. "I told them that I would converge lines of energy into a single point and from that single point I would create a door. Then I pushed everyone through the door," she smiled mischievously. The women laughed along with her.

My eyes widened, astounded. First, my dream from hours before sounded very close to the dreaming activities she had just described from the previous night. Second, I looked around me curiously and realized that these women were her apprentices. The Nagual had never used that term before, although she'd used the term "student" on Tuesday evenings in reference to those who attended.

"Hey, listen to my dream last night!" I offered, and excitedly relayed my dream. In the midst of recounting the dream, I glanced around at the women and made an immediate decision. I dropped the last part of the dream – the part where the Nagual jumped up and down and shouted, "I knew you could see them!" My relationship with these women and the Nagual was fresh and innocent like a sprout whose first leaf was unfolding with new life. Too much enthusiasm felt overwhelming, as though that same new sprout could wilt if exposed to too much heat in an afternoon sun. The Nagual glanced sharply my way but said nothing.

As we finished cleaning, the Nagual gathered us together.

"It's time to give Jessica a spirit guide to protect her during energetic travel," she announced. Turning to Suzanne, the Nagual directed, "Suzanne, the spirit animal will come to you. Tell Jessica what it is."

Suzanne didn't hesitate. Quickly, she answered, "Oh, I know what it is, it's right here, this close to your face." Suzanne held up her hand six inches away from my eyes. "It's a fox, a white one," she said. "It's mature, silent." She paused and then corrected herself. "Not silent, but subtle. It's maternal and nurturing. I'm not sure it has young ones, but it acts in a maternal way." Fox had never been an animal guide to me. In the past, my animal guide had always been Crow, so I was eager for this connection with an unfamiliar animal guide.

The use of animal guides is a common teaching tool in shamanism and on the Toltec path. The animal guides come in visions, and they also come in daily reality. Remember the crows that flew above my head while I stood in a condominium complex shortly before coming to Hawaii? The task for the student of these two disciplines is to familiarize herself with the animal, its characteristics, actions, and behaviors in the world. Through these avenues the animal guide provides potential knowledge on the path.

"Pay close attention to the energy of Fox," the Nagual instructed. "He will hover near you until you acquaint yourself with him."

I thanked Suzanne. I'd never met her before that morning, but I liked her immediately. She had an easy manner about her. While cleaning the Center, I'd observed how friendly and familiar she was with everyone, as though on a regular basis she casually dropped by their homes to say hi, or met them for a drink in the evening after a stressful day of work. She knew everyday things about the women that implied mutual friendships.

The women rose off the carpet where they'd been seated and began to gather their belongings. The Nagual motioned toward me with a slight movement of her head and indicated for me to follow her. As we walked out of earshot of the other women, the Nagual commented, "You're interested in becoming an apprentice."

I wasn't sure whether it was a question or a statement. I paused. The moment I'd been marshaling all of my actions toward for the past year was finally present. I hadn't seen it coming, so there was no butterfly stomach, no sweaty palms, no uneven breathing. The decision to come and study with the Nagual had been made a year ago, but the confirmation of that decision was in a nod of my head, a simple spoken word, "Yes." With all of my heart and soul, I was there to apprentice with this Nagual in the Toltec tradition. I nodded my affirmation.

"Then start coming on Tuesday and Thursday evenings." The Nagual turned to leave. See you next week for the massage." It was very nearly a question.

"I'll see you Saturday at eleven," I confirmed, as she handed me a slip of paper with her address scribbled on it.

December 31

On the last day of the year, I drove over to the neighborhood Laundromat to wash clothes. Discouraged, I kept going over and over finances in my head. I'd just been on the phone with my credit union in California to discover why several checks had been returned unpaid. It turned out that the old checks I'd used to pay several bills had been drawn on an account that had been closed for two years. How had I confused old checks with new ones and then used an account with no money in it? To further discourage me, Laurelle came home from school with the information that semester rates for her spring classes had all been raised. Good God! How was I going to pay for everything?

I carried the pillowcase stuffed with laundry inside. Once a week either Laurelle or I brought our laundry to this little neighborhood dive because our place didn't have a washing machine or a dryer. I hated putting my clothes into a washing machine that'd been used by strangers. There were always used dryer sheets, odd socks, and an occasional wine bottle littering the floor. A lone sink stood at the back of the dump, full of lint, loose hair, and who-knew-what, and the corner of the room reeked of urine. And for sure the only washer that wasn't spinning had someone's abandoned clothes stuffed into it. Did I have enough quarters for three loads? Nope! I was short three quarters.

Pushing extra clothes into the first two machines, thereby eliminating the need for washing three loads, I pulled a book from my purse to read while the clothes went through the wash cycle. I'd read the book before, but it was a habit of mine to grab a book if I were going anywhere, and to do a little reading if I had a few spare minutes. It was also a habit of mine to open the book randomly and begin to read.

As I opened the book and began reading, the words passed my eyes in slow motion, an exaggerated pace that was maddening as each word stood, saluted, and would not be denied its rightful position in the lineup. Why I was reading so slowly I didn't know, because the words had my full, undivided attention from the moment the book fell open. In fact, my attention was riveted on the words. Suddenly, I lowered the book and closed my eyes, leaning against the washing machine for support. The words might as well have been spoken through a megaphone. They were insistent and loud like Japanese Taiko drummers. They echoed in my ears and then disappeared. For a brief second, there was nothing inside me except a nine-ounce organ pounding in my chest for all it was worth.

Marching like soldiers in formation, the words rose off the page: "Taking responsibility means accepting everything you say, feel, hear, write, see, and communicate as part of you."

A space opened up inside my mind, a space I had never known existed until I had learned to slow my thinking to a standstill. It was a blank slate, an empty mind swept clean of thoughts, beliefs, or emotions. Profoundly silent, just like the first few moments of quiet when the Taiko drums stopped their beating, its awareness was outside every bit of knowledge and information that I knew. In the moment I stood, facing the row of dryers directly across from the washing machines with book in hand; I wanted the space of profound silence to stay longer. All too quickly it filled with the image of The Tower in my Tarot deck – destruction, downfall, even death. I opened my eyes and turned back to the book so that The Tower would disappear from my mind, and continued to read.

"Accepting your accidents and your lies is an act of compassion. Taking responsibility means that if you are sick, you must understand that the body is bringing up a dream you have not yet known. If you have relationship difficulties, accidents, or world problems, things are happening to you with which you are not in agreement."[2]

Wait a minute! What had I been thinking moments before

reading those words? Because when words stand out as though they're shouting at me as I read them, there's a connection between the written words and the immediate moment I'm experiencing. That moment contains Power because it contains no duality; it is a moment of direct connection and unity between internal and external experience. "Power" is a clear mind and a direct connection with the energy of the Universe. What had I been thinking as I put my dirty laundry into dirty washing machines? Ahh! I'd been worrying about money and hating the fact that I was at a Laundromat! Then I'd exaggerated my thoughts about money by complaining that money issues were hanging over me like a heavy thundercloud, always on the verge of drowning me. But the words on that page had channeled my complaints in a different direction and I hadn't seen it coming. I wasn't in agreement with my attitude about money, was I? What were my money issues saying to me?

I pulled the clothes from the washing machine, then spun around and stuffed them into two open dryers. The answer to my question arrived like a bullet train going 180 miles per hour, screeching to a halt directly in front of the dryer door: I was a victim to my ideas on the value of money! I'd never seen it before! And if I flipped that coin, the ramifications of having money astounded me: If I had money, I would no longer have money problems to focus my attention on. I would have fewer bills and therefore pay all of them on time, and I would be an upstanding financial citizen. I would give more to charitable organizations, I would have my retirement sitting in a 401k, and my daughters wouldn't have one school loan to their name.

Uppermost, if I had money I wouldn't spend so much wasted energy on trying to resolve my financial dilemma, and the lack of three quarters wouldn't put me into a tailspin. But because I didn't have money, that gave me the excuse to do what I did, to worry, to rob Peter to pay Paul, to finagle, to squander energy in a pattern that was all too familiar. My financial actions were telling me, "Be responsible! Drop the victim stance that says you can be irresponsible because you don't have money. Redirect your energy."

At the precise moment a period was put onto that last thought, a large smoky black butterfly fluttered across my eyes. Directly in front of me, directly in front of the dryer door, the butterfly floated along on silken sails. Beautiful, velvet, carefree, its presence an agreement from spirit, an agreement that beliefs about money kept me a prisoner to their binding energy. My beliefs about money needed to shape-shift in a drastic way, to transform from a chrysalis to a winged creature. This alone would have been enough upheaval, but The Tower of my beliefs kept tumbling.

The Nagual's way of looking at the Toltec path was different than mine. In the short while that I'd been listening to her lectures and attending weekend activities, I'd discovered that our emphasis on walking the Toltec path was very different. When she spoke of love as the driving force on the Toltec path, I was frustrated, but it was not only her language that confused me. When she didn't respond well to my questions, I was stymied. When her communication was short and cryptic, I longed to hear more. It had been several months since first immersing myself into her point of view. Previous years had been spent walking the Toltec path alone – with books, yes, but without active engagement with others. How much did I cling to being a lone Toltec? Could I shift my perspective to a group approach directed by this Nagual? My ability to be flexible in my thought was on the line, wasn't it?

Those questions challenged me because I wasn't convinced of the answers. I opened the dryer and pulled out the warm, static-filled clothes. Placing them in the laundry basket, I carried them over to a large table and dumped them. I folded them mindfully, as though doing so was the only thing I had to concern myself with at the moment, glad of the heat that would put creases and folds in just the right places. A moment's rest from the structures of thought falling around me felt comforting. The clothes were in neat, warm piles before I dared return my attention to my belief systems about money and the Nagual.

The demand for transformation was crystal clear and devastating at the same time. If my view on money could shift and transform (and indeed it must!), if my mood determined what I did with money, and that mood needed to be eliminated, my expectations for who a Nagual was and what a Nagual did also needed to transform.

My expectations were that I would be able to grasp what she was teaching but I did not always understand. The manner with which she described Toltec concepts was strange to me. If written language were enough, I could have remained in California and simply read the Nagual's book, but I had come to Hawaii to initiate a face-to-face journey on the Toltec path. If language became a barrier, I would overcome it. I was there to learn from this Nagual, and since she taught in a manner that was unfamiliar and even uncomfortable, I would need to make adjustments in order to remain open to her teaching.

I glanced over at the butterfly as it looped in flight, up, over, and around the laundry machines. Silently, I gave it thanks. Grabbing my clean clothes and laundry detergent, I stuffed them into the back seat of the car. While not yet able to articulate it clearly, Death had paid me a visit. The death of my expectations on a teacher and my ideas around money issues were real and no less significant than if those expectations and ideas had been flesh and blood. Climbing into the car, I realized it was the last day of the year, an omen in its own way. A new year was coming and with it the birth of a new journey.

Part Two: North

– The direction of knowledge and wisdom that arrives amidst a time of discomfort and trouble. In the cold North, we go within to warm our soul.

The challenge in the North is to transform the roles and relationships in our lives in order to become the author of our own story.

January 22

The foster parent was adamant: the kid was smoking pot. He knew it because he'd asked him outright, "Are you smoking pakalolo?"

When alone with Keola, he confirmed the same story. "Yes, I smoke weed, but only when I'm stressed, like when he is on me about my homework," and he nodded his head toward the other room where his foster father waited in order to give us privacy while we talked.

My job as the foster agency therapist was to provide counseling services to foster parents and to the children placed in their homes. Keola was like many of the youth I'd already met at the agency. He was part Hawaiian, without family to care for him, struggling in school due to lack of interest, and had a preoccupation with more than a decade of family neglect before being placed in a foster home. Smoking marijuana came with the territory for this kid.

On my drive back to the office, I reflected on how the agency had only one policy on substance use, but that policy was already a moot point with this family. I was eager to speak with the program supervisor, Marianne. She'd recently been promoted to supervisor having held the position that I now held as the agency therapist. The stance that the agency had regarding substance use and the foster youths was unfamiliar to me. I'd been uncertain as to how to advise Keola's foster father, and Marianne would direct me, I was certain.

Marianne looked at me as I walked into the small agency office on the second floor in downtown Waipahu. The look on my face was all she needed to know that something was wrong. She motioned me into her office and closed the door.

"Keola's smoking weed again," I sighed. She heard the implication of my short statement and sighed herself. "The agency takes a hands-off approach about drug use," she reminded me. "The program states that the kids we take are to be clean when they come into the program, and making sure they aren't actively using is part of the assessment. If they relapse, we have no resource within the agency that specifically addresses the problem."

I stared at her, appalled at the agency's reasoning, before saying, "Then we're shooting ourselves in the foot because the majority of the kids that come into the program are chronic users. If we take them in, looking the other way while they continue to use, then it's only a matter of time before their drug abuse escalates, particularly at the level of drug use I've seen so far in these youths." My voice was rising.

I wanted to understand the rationale for providing clinical services to adolescents that didn't address their drug use. Explaining that it isn't agency policy begs the issue. Debating whether or not substance abuse is the cause or effect amongst the laundry list of challenges these kids face didn't placate me either.

"It's not an area we can programmatically address," Marianne reiterated. She sounded tired. "The kids we take have no place else to go; they're the unwanted kids of Hawaii. Whether or not we address the drug use isn't consequential because it isn't going to be addressed any other place either."

Marianne was a small Japanese woman whose focused movements in the office spelled efficiency, professionalism, and a thorough understanding of agency policies. But at the moment Marianne's tone of voice reminded me of the airline stewardess on the plane from California to Hawaii, the tone of indifference after having repeated the same "lifesaving oxygen mask" too many times.

I choked, tears welling up in my eyes. "You know that if their drug use isn't addressed, nothing else we do is going to matter." I was appealing to Marianne's higher education and her emotions in a single sweep. Now it was my voice that sounded tired.

"Do you know how many times I've had this conversation with new employees from out of state?" Marianne parried. "People who move to Hawaii do it for all of the positive things the island offers, but there's a negative side that comes with it, and they're not prepared to see the downside of paradise. I come into this office, shut the door, and scream with the same frustration you have." Marianne finally sounded as though she was running a business that involved human lives.

"Thanks for the speech," I nodded weakly.

"Come in and let it all out anytime," she said without a trace of sarcasm.

I had begun to track my emotional reactions as of late. When an emotional reaction was that strong, it was usually evidence of a strong attachment to an idea. Generally, that idea was in charge of me rather than the other way around, just as was the case with my view on money. The combination of a strong belief with an even stronger emotion made for an impenetrable force that drove behavior, with little appeal to the actual experience at hand. This driving of behavior with values and beliefs unrelated to daily reality was the duality I longed to do away with. I wanted my inner world to align with my outer world, rather than to experience the disconnect I so often felt between the two of them.

I questioned myself on the drive home: *Look, Jessica, get real. You broke into tears over a fourteen-year-old who is smoking weed. What's going on?*

Yes, the agency criterion that addresses substance use is unfamiliar to you. California places high value, demand even, on addressing drug use in the adolescent population in residential care. Yes, you'll return to the foster father and youth and give them the resources that the state of Hawaii provides, albeit scanty in your opinion. Yes, the people of Hawaii have a different attitude about how they view social, political, cultural, and educational issues, all of which are new to you. These things contribute to your aching spirit. Remember, you're still adjusting to your move here.

The drive home was forty-five minutes. On an island that took only seventy minutes to drive at its greatest longitude, even less on the latitude, this meant I was sitting in traffic. I was not opposed to sitting in traffic (years of driving in Orange County were not yet a distant memory); in fact, it had always been a good time and place for me to reflect.

Emotions are tricky, I reminded myself. *They're not real.*

The previous Thursday evening the Nagual had spoken about how our emotions were a contrivance of the mind. She'd said, "They build a reputation in our psyche, and then we act as though we owe them allegiance. They gain such an honored place in our self-concepts that we begin to lose the realization that they're not who we really are. Deeper than our emotions are our feelings. Our feelings are part and parcel of our body physiology. What is confusing is the difference between emotions and feelings."

Whenever her words cycled with me for days, I knew to pay attention to them. "Everything is a symbol, even emotions," spoke the Nagual. "They are simply energy that wants to be expressed." I'd spoken up as soon as she paused.

"But the word 'symbol' signifies an action of the mind because it implies representation. Our minds automatically interpret a symbol by giving meaning to it, and then it's no longer about energy but about meaning. I thought we wanted to work with energy, not meaning."

"You're looking at it from a mental perspective; what else could a symbol stand for?" The Nagual spoke sharply.

"I don't know," I answered lamely. Suddenly, I couldn't think in order to take the conversation to the next step. The very thing the Nagual wanted me to see, the connection between the emotions and the mind, blocked me from responding.

"A symbol can also stand for feelings. You're coming from the mind, Jessica. You need to get out of the mind and work from the level of your feelings." The Nagual shifted her attention to the group.

"Emotions are treated as though they're naughty but they're not. They are energy in motion. We are the ones to attribute a positive or negative value to them. Feelings, which are a lot less complicated than emotions, will tell us who we really are."

Still stinging from the Nagual's comment, I lay down on the carpet quickly and shut my eyes as we got ready for the evening meditation. The singing bowl began to vibrate, and as it did the volume rose higher and higher. I placed all of my attention on my *tantien*, "the location of our feelings," the Nagual had said. The tantien was the center of the energy body and was located two finger lengths below the navel at the center of the physical body.

It took some time for me to feel my tantien in order to identify my feelings. My emotions were recoiling at my embarrassment after the exchange with the Nagual. Not only was I embarrassed due to our exchange, but I also was left without a clear understanding of my interactions with the Nagual. When I asked questions it was as though I was challenging her. With tremendous effort I paid attention to my feelings rather than my interaction with the Nagual. My feelings were unruffled; they were calm.

Yes, you're in your head, Jessica, I confirmed to myself. *It's a familiar place for you to be. Remember, when you react emotionally to a comment, that comment has hooked you and reveals the high value you've placed on whatever is being said. When there is a neutral reaction, you can be assured that you're not carrying around emotional baggage.*

The Nagual said you're in your head and you agree with her, by the force of your internal reaction. Although they appear opposed to each other, the Nagual's comment and your reaction are actually aligned. One is a statement and the other is negating the same statement, in reality making a positive and a negative statement on an agreement. Yes, you walked yourself through the interaction from a psychological stance, but what about your feelings? What about your energy at this moment?

I got it! Finally the two came together while sitting in stop and go traffic on the H1 Freeway driving into Honolulu. I had overreacted emotionally to a social service agency that didn't value drug intervention. They weren't addressing the issue like I wanted them to, and expected they should.

I also overreacted emotionally to the Nagual, taking her observations of my intellect personally. The snag in my communication with her occurred on an emotional level, leaving me to miss what she was trying to teach me. I needed to let those emotionally charged situations go and realize that they didn't identify or determine who I was, either as a therapist to adolescent kids smoking marijuana or as an apprentice learning from the Nagual.

Once again, I saw that whenever I overreacted, it revealed that my emotions were taking charge. In this case, when I checked in with my feelings, they told me that I was exactly where I needed to be, both as a therapist and as an apprentice.

January 31

White Fox began to show up in my meditations and journeys, moving across the dreamscape in silence. Once I asked him outright, "What are you here for?" I didn't mean to be rude; I just didn't know what he was up to. I remembered his role as protector, but I didn't understand what he was protecting me from.

"Some energies you may encounter are not in your best interest," White Fox instructed. "I will help you determine the difference between those energies. I will also teach you about silence."

White Fox appeared once again at the Candlemas ceremony that marks the beginning of spring, midway between the winter solstice and the spring equinox. The Nagual read the history of the ceremony. In general, she emphasized the ceremony's association with the element of fire and, in particular, she emphasized the cleaning of fire's aftermath: a hearth full of ashes.

The Nagual gave the eight women in the circle instructions for the evening's mirror meditation, something she usually left for us to determine on our own. The question we were to ask ourselves: "What do you want to clear from the hearth in order to relight the coming year's hearth fire?"

Standing amidst the mirrors, my eyes were closed, as I stood back-to-back with three other women. My mind jumped to the most obvious giveaway as we settled into the meditation. What I wanted to clear from the hearth was my attitude about money. If the belief about money were swept away, then the constant worry about money would also go. My belief about money was through the lens of lack; I acted as though I never had enough money because that was my belief. The topic was a slam-dunk. It'd been hovering around my psyche for several months and I was ready to let it go.

"That's it then," I concluded. But the image that presented itself didn't have anything to do with money. A heat was beginning to slowly rise up my legs from my feet, radiating through my torso and my arms. I watched the flames, the source of the rising temperature in the room, licking up and around my legs.

Squirming, I bumped into the women on either side of me, forgetting that I was standing in a circle with others during a meditation. Calming myself, I murmured apologies to the two women on either side. The fire wavered, slowly forming a question mark with my flaming body.

A question mark? Questions! What? Give up questions?

The silence in the void confirmed my suspicions. The fire extinguished. White Fox appeared and trotted across my interior field of vision, saying nothing. The meditation was over.

Immediately, I began to debate my experience (as if debating an experience ever changed it). How could I possibly give up asking questions? Besides, I was in good company; Castaneda asked a million questions. There was no wrong question, right?

"Anyone want to share about their meditation?" the Nagual invited. Instantly the heat returned. If I said nothing, the meditation would go away externally, but internally it wouldn't digest, like an eight-ounce steak sitting in the stomach. If I said something, I would feel bound to what I said, as though making an agreement between the group and myself. Wavering in the agony of indecision, my internal temperature rose. My mouth opened before I was cognizant a decision had been made.

"I'm going to give up asking questions."

The heat disappeared like drops of rain hitting warm asphalt. There was no point in doing meditations if I ignored what happened while I was in them, I reasoned. I wanted to explain further, to tell the group that asking questions helped to sort information in my head, but suddenly it became clear that the overload of the questions I asked simply filled my head with more information that needed sorting in turn. That perspective had never occurred to me before.

For the life of me, though, I couldn't fathom not asking questions. Questions were the rudder that steered the boat; they were the steering wheel that directed the car's travel. Thoughts and beliefs were run through an assembly line of questions like a bushel of potatoes being sorted for size and firmness. They helped organize my thoughts, feelings, and beliefs. Without them I was convinced I couldn't understand what was happening.

My mouth clamped shut. Suddenly, changing my beliefs and value on money seemed like the easier route to pursue; yet it wasn't the issue White Fox had indicated for me to take.

"Understanding?" White Fox spoke quietly. "Is that what you want? To understand? To always demand understanding is a mind game."

I was familiar with asking questions, but I'd never, dare I say, questioned my motives for asking them, nor whom I asked the questions of. Why, already in the space of thirty seconds I'd asked myself half a dozen questions. If I were no longer going to ask the Nagual questions, then I no longer needed to ask myself the same barrage of questions.

This was the energy that White Fox had alluded to at the beginning of the ceremony – the energy that I needed to protect myself from – my own internal pressure and drive to understand what was happening to me through the guise of asking questions. The answers to my questions provided me information but not knowledge. Knowledge came through silence, through the Void, where questions were irrelevant. Brushing aside questions that lie on my heart's hearth was the task at hand. The only way to gain silence was to go within, and going within was the lesson to learn in the North on the medicine wheel.

February 2, Morning

The next day, on the telephone with my daughter in New York, I unloaded frustrations that had been building for some time.

"Carla, I don't get it. When I go in the evenings to listen to the Nagual, by the time I get home, I'm annoyed. I don't know if it's the other apprentices, or if it's something about her or something about me, but I'm agitated every time I come home."

"Mom, have you said anything to her?" Carla queried.

"What do you suggest I say, 'You annoy me'?"

Hearing the sarcasm in my voice reminded me of White Fox's task to teach me silence. The guilt of feeling annoyed and judgmental was what drove my sarcasm. Before coming to Hawaii, I'd never considered that the relationship between a student and a teacher would be laced with so much agitation. And if agitation was present, surely I was in a position to do something about it, but what?

Odd that I hadn't recognized the dynamic in the developing relationship between the Nagual and me, given that the relationship between Castaneda and Don Juan was conflictive – as described by both of them in so many of Castaneda's books – and loaded with a contrariness that was palpable. Don Juan told Castaneda on one occasion that he felt revulsion toward him as an apprentice, and Castaneda responded with self-pity, as he often did when challenged. But then again, who wants to be told they're obnoxious and self-centered?

"I'm here to study with the Nagual," I told Carla. "I'm clear on that much. I'm complaining to you but I haven't said anything to anyone else. I want to learn as much as I can and – "

"What are you learning?" Carla interrupted.

"I'm learning just how attached I am to Castaneda. The Nagual has such a different take on the Toltec path. It's like they have different styles of clothing, and I'm moaning because she wears linen and he wore polyester. Many of their concepts are similar. Last week I told her I would stop asking questions. I need to take in what she's saying instead of constantly asking questions. Otherwise, I feel like I'm stuck always trying to cross-reference what she says with Castaneda."

"Mom, you know being attached to Castaneda isn't what you want. Allegiance to him doesn't prove anything. But you love his words and their familiarity. Go easy on yourself. You're learning a new language."

"I visited Castaneda again," I said. It sounded like a confession. In the past year during my meditation times, I had traveled to a cave and Castaneda had met me by a small fire. He'd sat and smoked a pipe, while I'd sat alongside him with a small twig fire burning in the shallow sand between us, a wisp of red smoke spiraling up the open space to the ceiling. Others communed with Jesus or with Buddha, and my point of contact with a great teacher who had passed on was Carlos Castaneda.

"I finally asked him what happened," I continued. Finally, I had been able to stay in the cave long enough, to get up enough courage, to ask what had long perplexed me, a mystery that millions of people had also wondered about: what happened at the end of Castaneda's life? News reports said he died of cancer. What had happened to Castaneda that he hadn't "burned with the fire within," dissolved into complete awareness, and launched himself out of this world? It wasn't a mystery that it was really the Nagual Don Juan's teachings that had always gripped me most, those teachings that Castaneda had recorded in all of his books; but for some inexplicable reason I gave my allegiance to Castaneda. I loved the messenger nearly as much as I loved the message.

"When I asked him about the circumstances that had happened at the end of his life, he answered, 'I didn't...'" and then he didn't finish the sentence, as though it wasn't necessary. Weird, huh?" I finished hurriedly as though if I didn't speak quickly I might not say it at all. Even with my two daughters I felt self-conscious. Plenty of people talked to dead people; I had just never counted myself among them.

"You asked a question..." Carla spoke softly, her voice trailing to a stop. No accusation, no confrontation, nothing but a gentle statement.

I froze. If I'd been a deer crossing a busy roadway, I would've been dead. Tears burst from my eyes, and I lowered the cell phone. Moments elapsed as Carla waited and I stared at the wall in front of me.

"You're right," I confessed. "I did what I always do – ask questions so that I could understand. If I was in tune with what my heart was saying rather than my head, I wouldn't have to ask so many questions." I muffled a sob.

"But Castaneda did what he always did, too," Carla replied. "He negated, he denied, he acted as though he couldn't be responsible for himself." I was shocked at seeing myself so clearly revealed from Carla's statement.

"Both Castaneda and I use language that supports our worldview," I whispered softly, seeing this comparison between us for the first time. We emphasize words as a means to learn about the path, rather than to grasp that experience was of greater value than the words used to describe those same experiences.

Carla continued as I walked into the bathroom for Kleenex to wipe the tears from my face. "One thing I'm learning in my program is that I know things through my body. My movement class is all about how our bodies know how to act if we know our bodies. The trouble is that so many people don't know their body. Fits in with Toltec thinking, doesn't it?"

"And you, Mom, you focus on words. You identify how you know things by how you can explain them in words. Both ways teach us but they limit us if they become exclusive."

She continued. "Castaneda did burn with the fire within. (The alignment of the Tonal and the Nagual into one perception that concludes in leaving this world.) We all do, in the end. But this reality labeled him as 'dying of cancer.' The purpose of this body, of this life, is to live totally and fully, without all of the restrictions our minds place on the experience. All of us will end up at the same place in the end – and it's not heaven or hell – it's movement from one conscious experience to another. The universe is about awareness and our awareness supersedes our birth and follows our death. We return to awareness at death, conscious of it or not."

Her conviction left me speechless. All of my wrangling about words left me preoccupied with a focus that misdirected me away from my purpose of aligning the Tonal and the Nagual in a state of non-duality. The North winds of my journey were blowing hard. It was time to shift my perspective.

February 2, Evening

Lying on the bed after arriving home from work, I closed my eyes. What a grueling day it had been! The day had dragged on as though waiting for water to boil on the stove. The foster father, with the foster son, Keola, called the office requesting to have him removed from the home. It hadn't been more than a month before since he'd called and asked to adopt the same kid. Now, he wanted him removed immediately. Being a foster parent for these kids was not an easy thing. Neither was it easy being the therapist. Marianne was right; these were tough kids.

As the thoughts about the day lessened, I adjusted my body to a comfortable position. I lay on the bed on my back, legs straight, arms at my side. This familiar position signaled that I was going on a shamanic journey. Even without the headphones and the CD playing, my body settled into the routine position and mindset. My breathing slowed down, my body calmed, and my heart rate adjusted accordingly.

"Ah, I'll lie here in silence," I murmured, as though someone were listening. At other times, I had used active imagination, but this time I needed the calmness and peacefulness provided by the blank screen of silence. I had the house all to myself. Unexpectedly, unsolicited, White Fox appeared.

"Questions are distracting," White Fox began, getting right to the point for his visit. "They distance you from what is happening in the moment. When you ask questions, they direct your energy away from the moment. You don't allow yourself the opportunity to be fully present in the dynamics of what is happening before you. They act in the same way as your body used to when you first began going on these journeys. Remember? Your body used to twitch and itch. You used to feel tightness in odd places, and you'd end up squirming around. All of that movement made it difficult to focus your energy. Now you lie down and get into a meditative state quickly without your body movements to bother and distract you."

Eagerly, I reported to White Fox: "I told the Nagual I was not going to ask any more questions after the last mirror meditation." I felt encouraged by what White Fox was telling me. The information he was sharing aligned with the recent meditation. "And you were going to teach me about silence," I reminded him.

"Yes. Letting go of questions will go a long way toward gaining inner silence," White Fox assured me. "The two are linked in a way you've not been aware of before now." And then a moment later, he was gone. *Damn, he's fast,* I thought. Of course, if he'd hung around any longer I would have asked him a question (it was proving to be a difficult habit to break).

My body was still. All was dark and quiet. Whenever I did not feel my body, I was free of it. This completely relaxed state opened me to what Robert Monroe called a "rote," or a bundle of knowledge that comes all at once as though our cognitive thought process is not needed for the acquisition of the knowledge. The bundle just appears fully grown, generated by the dark void.[3] In an instant, boom! The rote is there within the silent mind.

Strangely, the rote had little to do with posing questions. Instead, it dealt with two important Toltec concepts called Power and Dreaming. The download of knowledge didn't provide description or definition; that was for me to determine, and I had a beginner's grasp on the two terms.

Power is the fuel needed to run the physical and etheric bodies. A goal for an apprentice on the Toltec path is to acquire Power, a clear mind and direct connection with universal energy, so that the physical and etheric bodies run efficiently. The apprentice can practice techniques that will increase his or her Power. Dreaming is one of those techniques. Dreaming in the Toltec sense is to be aware of the function of dreams, and consequently to use them volitionally in an active rather than passive manner. Dreaming as an activity is not to be confused with nighttime dreams. Nighttime dreams are the subconscious means for dealing with psychic issues as opposed to lucid dreaming, using the dream as fuel for the energy body.

The download of knowledge came quickly: the only purpose dreams served energetically was to increase Power, otherwise they consumed the dreamer with details and acted as distractions to energy, much like questions do. But a dream is not significant unless one can wield Power in it. This is the difference between dreams and Dreaming. Dreams are to the night what daily activities are to the day. The details of our dreams and the details in our daily lives prevent us from living clearly and powerfully in the present, if they are not recognized for what they really are.

A rote comes with no sense of time. In other words, it comes like downloading a zip file. Nothing is there, and then *click!*, suddenly the knowledge is fully present as though it's been there all along. It's difficult to account for how it happens so quickly and intensely.

The sensation of being in "the Void" and receiving a rote is like being in an elevator on the top floor when the ground floor button gets pushed. The downward motion feels like your stomach is dropping rapidly while the rest of your body is trying to keep up with the transition. Some people describe the sensation of being in another location energetically and then returning to the physical body as one of going through a tunnel. For me, it has always felt like an elevator ride. Regardless of the sensation, once it occurs the mind becomes active again about the same time you reach the ground floor.

Because of the download of knowledge on Power and Dreaming, I suddenly grasped with unerring accuracy what Don Juan had meant when he'd repeatedly dismissed Carlos Castaneda's phantasmagorical dreams. The dreams themselves are not of upmost importance to one following this path; they are just the "bells and whistles." It is tempting for the dreamer to get caught up in the wild experience of Dreaming and then to focus on the elements of the dream in this way. The *awareness* of the dreamer while Dreaming and where that awareness gets directed are functionally the most important aspects of the act of Dreaming, not the plotline or story that unfolds.

I can't answer the question why Carlos Castaneda asked Don Juan so many questions. Certainly, his questions felt distracting when reading his books. And I'd used his habit of questioning to support my own barrage of questions. "There's no dumb question," was the defense often used. But White Fox had made it very clear: "Asking questions clogged the conduit for the movement of Power into your life." And gaining Power allowed me to view the world and myself in it from the perspective of non-duality, with a clear mind and in direct connection with the energy of the Universe. All these ways of being in the world were the reasons why I'd come to Hawaii in the first place: they were the freedom I longed for.

February 8

"You guys are too damn polite," the Nagual complained. "Where's the emotion?"

The Nagual's eyes were full of fire, vim, and vinegar. The evening was nearly at an end, as she wrapped up her talk with a blatant accusation pointed at the group seated in front of her. "Seems to me this group has become complacent. Everyone's emotions around here are too flat."

Wide-eyed, I stared at the Nagual. She was unleashing a passion I'd not seen up til then. She spoke of the danger of lethargy, and the numbing effect our daily lives have on the etheric body. She spoke of emotions as energy in motion, nothing more and nothing less. She spoke of the tendency to block emotions at the expense of the expression of spirit. She spoke on and on, her body in rhythm with the words flowing from her mouth.

Galvanized, my heart pounded with the waves of electricity radiating off her body and magnified in her voice. This was the Nagual I had come to apprentice with! I knew it in every cell of my body.

"When I have permission, which I do from some of you, I will begin to push you. I will push you beyond your comfort zone. Blocked emotions rigidify the etheric body; emotions that flow freely make the etheric body fluid. In dreaming, I will come to you and work with your energy body; but I find that when I have your conscious consent, the energy work goes more smoothly. We have all gotten too comfortable. It's time for change."

I approached the Nagual immediately after her lecture. "Please," I consented, "you have permission to push me. Tell me what you see in me that I need to pay attention to." I wanted her to push me in order for my etheric body to become more fluid. Doing so would help clear the way for a more direct link with

Intent, which in turn would allow for more Power to be present in my life.

Standing close to her, I could feel her blue energy. It had happened several times before. Standing next to her during a meditation or speaking with her before or after class, I would see, inside my mind's eye, the color blue. Tonight the blue was vibrant, alive, and pulsing with electricity. I told her what I saw. The Nagual smiled, saying nothing.

Later, it was nearing midnight and I couldn't sleep. I felt like I'd had one too many Red Bulls. Rather than agitation, though, I felt ebullient. This was the state of being that had always propelled me on freedom's road.

Recently the agency had sent me to a workshop that focused on systems – systems as a model of addressing human behavior in relationships. The Human Resource Department was making a concerted effort to get management employees to raise their level of awareness about just how powerfully a system determined behavior within a group. For me, the correlations between the workshop information on group dynamics and what occurred in the Tuesday and Thursday evenings with the Nagual were intriguing.

The workshop emphasized that whether we liked it or not, whether we were aware of it or not, once we became a member of a group our behavior was influenced by the norms, expectations, and assumptions held by the collective members of that group.

By that time, I had belonged to the Nagual's group of students and apprentices for two months. As a therapist looking from a psychological point of view, I had observed the dynamics evident in the group, and I hadn't always liked what I saw. My observations were that the group of women would often approach the Nagual as though she were a counselor, speaking to her of their relationship issues or communication concerns. I also observed that the Nagual contributed to these quasi-counseling interactions and acted as a pseudo-therapist. Except that she wasn't a therapist. And by being involved in the group during these times, I was involved in dynamics that were more appropriate to a counselor's office than a group of apprentices studying with a Nagual.

In all my reading on the Toltec path, including Carlos Castaneda's books, there had been little reference to how a group functioned with a Nagual. The only group I was familiar with was Don Juan's apprentices, and they didn't get along with each other; in fact, they would have just as easily thrown each other under the proverbial bus than to be associated with one another. I also read of apprentices being challenged to compete with one another, and I wanted nothing to do with those dynamics. Other references to Naguals and their apprentices dealt with a one-on-one approach, rather than group dynamics.

I was relieved that the Nagual was on to some of the group dynamics occurring right under her nose, at least what I surmised she meant by the group being "too damn polite" and complacent. From my observation as a group member, the group often spoke amongst themselves of daily events and interactions, and little of their aspirations and endeavors as Toltec apprentices. But then again, the Nagual wasn't clear on the shenanigans she referred to; it was left to each one of us to apply her exhortations "if the shoe fit." For my part, I was excited for her to "push" me. As soon as I was able to sleep, I would watch for her in my dreams.

February 23

A large amethyst crystal adorned one corner of the Nagual's meeting place. Standing over two feet tall and nearly a foot wide, the crystal was shaped like a gaping crevice open to inspection, wider at the center, tapered to a point at the tip-top, and cut horizontal at the base in order for it to stand on a flat surface. The piece had been in the corner for as long as I'd been coming on Tuesday and Thursday evenings, but this was the first evening I'd noticed it. "Noticed" meaning that, as I glanced over in that general direction during the Nagual's talk on filter systems that particular evening, I saw two eyes peering back at me from the depth of the crystal facets. Yep, there they were, two sparkling eyes about mid-level in the interior of the piece, staring straight at me. "That's right, I'm talkin' to you!" they announced.

A sense of non-duality was present: the Nagual was speaking about "filter systems" and I was conversing with a stone. For many people, the idea of speaking with an inanimate object would prevent them from speaking with a stone because of their filter system (i.e. their belief that "stones don't communicate with human beings"), but I was convinced that the stone had motioned for me to pay attention.

I turned back to the Nagual in order to listen to what she was saying. "Filter systems lessen our connection with Intent. Remember Intent is the creative force that we tap into to guide our lives. If our connection with Intent isn't clear or we're not aware of it, we have less creative force available to us, and the way in which we view the world muddies the impact of that creative force. Here's the kicker: until we're aware of those filter systems, it's easy to believe we're looking at the world clearly when we are not. We believe that what we see and experience is what the world is all about. By changing our filter systems, we experience more of who we are at each and every moment."

"And by filter system you mean – " Barbara began before the Nagual interrupted her. I liked Barbara. Give her thirty seconds and she'd finish her thought. Her comments were careful and slowly articulated but always right in tune with the Nagual's topic for the evening. Consistently, she responded to the Nagual's evening talks by asking for clarification, staying on topic, and relating the things the Nagual was saying to her own life.

The Nagual finished Barbara's sentence curtly as though she begrudged the slowness with which Barbara spoke: " – the preferences, the likes and dislikes, the moods, the lens through which we choose to see life. We can change our filter systems so that we experience magic daily, if we so choose."

Barbara continued as though she hadn't noticed that the Nagual spoke for her. "Because I was wondering, if by filter system you also meant some of the healthy ways we view things in our lives, but you just said, 'the likes and dislikes,' didn't you?" Barbara had finally registered midstream what the Nagual had just said.

"Anything that keeps us from seeing the magic," the Nagual reiterated. "Magic is not a mysterious affair; it happens every day."

The urge to raise my hand and ask the Nagual what she meant by the word "magic" was strong. An exchange between the Nagual and I earlier in the week popped up on my mental screen. I had e-mailed the Nagual and told her about a dream that had shaken me up, shaken me so badly that I couldn't orient myself for a couple of days, as though I had landed on another planet and was clueless about my whereabouts. I'd lost my familiar way-of-being in the world – what a dream often does and what we want it to do on this path, truth be known – but the disorientation had lasted longer than it ever had before. I wanted the Nagual to clarify, not so much the dream elements, but my experience of extreme disorientation that had happened for days afterwards. The Nagual had e-mailed me back: "Might try just enjoying it."

She was doing the same thing again. Her comments were vague. For me the word "magic" meant sleight of hand and coins appearing behind people's ears. The way she used the term sounded different but begged for deeper explanation. It was as though a social studies student asked the science teacher how the sun rose in the sky each and every day, and the teacher responded, "It just does."

The purpose for coming Tuesday and Thursday evenings was not only for the Nagual to instruct and for us to listen, but also for discussion that took place as part of the practice for each evening. From my observation, however, the Nagual didn't like questions that honed in on the specifics of what she spoke, as though by asking clarifying questions we were really questioning the veracity of her words. She also responded a bit differently to each of the apprentices as they interacted with her. With Barbara, for instance, she was short-tempered and curt.

More group dynamics, I thought. *Stay out of them*, I reminded myself. *Yes, the Nagual treats everyone differently and that bothers you, but you don't want to get involved in everything you see swirling around in the group. You're here to learn from the Nagual, her teachings and her experiences.* However, since I couldn't understand the term "magic" and felt hesitant about getting clarification, I felt as uncertain as Barbara did.

I was in an odd juxtaposition. I observed, as though from the outside, the dynamics of what was occurring in the group of apprentices; and yet I was also a part of those same dynamics by virtue of simply being there. The workshop I'd attended on group dynamics was relevant to what the Nagual was saying, and the Nagual and the workshop facilitator were saying the same thing: it was difficult, if not impossible, *not* to be a participant-observer. By listening further to the Nagual, I saw how the belief that I was either a group member or not a group member was part of my filter system.

Once we join a system, and we join by virtue of being a participant in the group whether or not we speak up, we impact that system for better or for worse. I often found myself in between: I was part of the group and yet wasn't at the same time. I wanted to learn from the Nagual, but I didn't want to get caught up in the relational dynamics that I observed taking place. My desire to learn from the Nagual in conjunction with my hesitancy to become fully engaged with everyone so that I could stay focused on the teachings – both were in operation every evening as I sat down on the carpet along with everyone else for the evening's teaching.

Talk about disorientation and muddied filter systems! I couldn't keep the two of them from commingling, thus adding to my lack of clarity.

"Intent is not an abstract term; it is the manner in which our reality gets created," the Nagual was saying as my full attention returned from my musings. "What we see in front of us *is* Intent manifested. But…" the Nagual paused, "we see the view that confronts us through a filter as though we have on colored glasses. You've heard the term: 'Rose colored glasses'?"

"Yes," Suzanne affirmed, "it means we're seeing a situation from a jaded point of view."

"Intent is the creative force of the universe," the Nagual reiterated. "We use it to create our world, but it gets watered down, it gets jaded," and she nodded at Suzanne, "by the lens, the colored glasses, the filter system we use. Each one of us operates with filter systems; it's part of the human condition. But we operate as though we aren't responsible for those filter systems and we are." The Nagual paused, not for comments but for effect.

By filter system, the Nagual was referring to my beliefs, my expectations, and my assumptions, even how I used language to define my experience. What she was saying aligned with what

I'd learned in the workshop on systems. Not only did I impact the system or group I belonged to, but also that group or system had an equal impact on me.

"Any means we use to connect with Intent soon becomes part of our filter system," said the Nagual, continuing her lecture and developing the teaching on filter systems one step further. "We need to be on top of our filter systems so that they don't become dogma."

Suzanne spoke up again. "I understand the word 'dogma' from a religious perspective but how are you using it here?" It was the very question I longed to ask!

"When we begin to act in a routine manner without responding from the moment at hand, our behaviors are like a hamster on a wheel; they're on automatic pilot. When that occurs, we're responding to life without giving ourselves the option of choice. We've narrowed our options down to only one. We're responding in a predetermined manner. Whenever we respond in a predetermined manner, we curtail our freedom."

"Can you give us an example?" Suzanne inquired, voicing another question I would have asked had I been allowing myself to ask questions in my usual manner.

The Nagual posed a question in turn. "What happens to the dogs at home when I open the back door?" Everyone knew the Nagual had half a dozen cats and dogs. She spoke of them often and used their antics as points to drive home in her lectures.

"They immediately want to go out for a walk," Carol piped in without a trace of her usual sarcasm.

"Yes, they associate the door opening with going outside, even though my purpose for stepping out the door may not be to take the dogs out. Their doggy minds associate 'door' with 'outside,' and that's a filter system."

"So when Tom walks into the house in the evening with a bouquet of flowers, his filter system is saying 'sex'?" Carol was back to her usual humor.

"Not necessarily. I'd say that's *your* filter system," the Nagual retorted. Laughter erupted in the circle. "But that leads me to the last point on tonight's talk."

"Once we begin to see our own filter systems, we can begin to give ourselves choices as to how we respond to what is occurring in our lives. We also begin to realize that our filter systems interact with other people's filter systems. That's when our interactions get really interesting."

Taking a large crystal bowl from the altar, the Nagual placed it in the middle of the room, signaling that it was time for the evening's meditation. Everyone lay down on the carpet and positioned their heads facing toward the bowl in the center. The Nagual began to hit the drum and soon I was deep into a meditative state.

Suddenly, the amethyst crystal dominated the blank screen of my mind. The stone spoke, "Don't abandon yourself to anything."

Nonhuman consciousness was short and cryptic – at least, the interaction I'd had with it in the past few years sure had been. *Not far different from the Nagual,* I thought wryly. Throughout the rest of the meditation I wondered what "abandoning" myself meant. "Anything" sounded pretty inclusive to me.

After the meditation was over, the Nagual asked if anyone had any comments, as she did every night. I raised my hand.

"The amethyst crystal was eyeing me as you were speaking earlier this evening. During the meditation, it came to me with a message."

"What did the stone say?" The Nagual turned her head sharply, her electrifying blue eyes boring into me.

"It told me not to abandon myself to anything," I said quizzically, hoping my tone would prompt the Nagual to say more about the reason for her interest. As the group disbanded for the evening, the Nagual came over to me. "I got a message for you during the meditation also. It said the opposite of what I normally say. It told me that you need to trust. You need to surrender yourself to this group."

"The opposite of what you normally say…" My tone of voice invited her to elaborate. *No questions, Jess, no questions.* I was asking less questions of the Nagual although I shuddered at hearing her last comment. Surrendering myself to the group was exactly what I feared doing. How could I surrender myself to a group of women when I couldn't determine how committed they were to the path? At times I wondered why they came to the Nagual for teaching. And at times I wondered why the Nagual continued to teach them.

"Normally, I say, 'Don't trust me,' because when people trust me explicitly, they tend to set themselves, and me, up with an agenda. But you need to trust. I have no agenda with you. I'm here to allow you to trust."

Immediately, I went into internal question mode. What was the difference between "surrender" and "abandon"? The two words seemed close in meaning. The crystal had said, "Don't abandon" and the Nagual had said, "Surrender." I wasn't sure what the difference was between them; and anyway, would knowing the difference clear up my feeling of confusion? It seemed to me that one was saying the opposite of the other.

I walked home slowly, preoccupied with the events of the evening. Despite the winter season, temperatures were in the seventies, the air was balmy, and a light breeze cooled my feverish thoughts. For the past few months I had walked the distance from my home to the Nagual's center. Walking rather than driving my car helped me to prepare for the upcoming evening and then to debrief after the evening was over. The walk took nearly an hour, but the time was worth it. That night, I definitely needed to debrief – those two words, so close in definition, had me by the throat.

As I walked into the house, I saw Laurelle seated on her bed, textbooks laid out around her. (She was pleased to have a "new"

Craigslist bedroom set that we'd picked up over the weekend, therefore no longer needing to sleep on the massage table.) I poked my head in the door and shared with her what had happened during the evening. Finally, I asked, "What's the difference between 'abandon' and 'surrender'?" Laurelle paused for a moment, thinking.

"*Abandon* means to leave something without notice or explanation. *Surrender* means to let go, to humbly give in. Does that help, Mom?"

"Thanks, sweetie. I can't seem to grasp the difference between those two words tonight. I'll give it more thought tomorrow." I hugged her and murmured good night.

Her definitions, although accurate, didn't aid in my grasp on the events of the evening. Why did the crystal direct me not to give myself over to anything and the Nagual direct me to give myself over to the group? Neither word was clear, not their definitions nor their relevance for me. Those two words, common in the English language, suddenly became mysterious when applied to events of the evening.

The North winds of change continued to blow, as I listened to the Nagual's lectures each evening. It would take a few years for me to grasp the difference between abandon and surrender as they related to my walk on the Toltec path with the Nagual. Eventually, as I gained a greater degree of clarity on the two terms, I came to understand that the amethyst was saying, "You don't need to abandon yourself to another set of ideologies as you are wont to do. Remember your experience in the church and in the practice of psychotherapy. Those were belief systems, or filter systems, that you immersed yourself into, and that is not what is necessary or expedient for you to do here with the Nagual.

At the same time, the Nagual was saying, "Set aside your own beliefs and ideas about this path and join us wholeheartedly in order for you to learn during your presence with us."

In the moment that the Nagual had given me her message for the evening, I had expected her to provide me with an understanding of the phrase, "Surrender yourself…" But doing so was not her teaching style. She provided lectures and activities and expected that each apprentice would process their own definitive journey. This teaching style left me frustrated, but it also drove me to define the journey for myself, something I was on my way to doing.

March 17

The weekend was to be my first off-island retreat with the Nagual. Ten of us had flown from Oahu to Hawaii, or "the Big Island," as it's known to the people of Hawaii. Two additional people, a couple, were flying in from the Midwest to join us for the weekend. The Nagual had arranged a bed and breakfast in the volcano fields midway between Hilo and Kona, a central location for easy travel during the workshop days. After settling into our lodging Friday night, we planned on rising early Saturday morning to head for Mauna Kea, the inactive volcano on the Big Island that is home to thirteen observatories from around the world. Our destination was a hike to a glacial lake that is sacred to the Hawaiian people, along the slope of the volcanic mountain Mauna Kea.

We packed into two vans and drove for nearly an hour to the 12,000-foot level of the mountain. In order to acclimatize to the high altitude, we browsed the small gift shop for another hour. We were also acclimatizing to temperatures in the low thirties. For those of us living on Oahu, this was extreme weather. After informing us that there was heavy fog higher on the mountain, the gift shop cashier was helpful by providing directions. "Look for the second parking area on the right, park, and then hike toward the left. Over a small decline in the mountain you'll find the glacial lake." A mystical lake, whereabouts unknown, extreme temps and heavy fog: my kind of adventure!

The drive was slow. The vans were loaded and chug chugging in the altitude. Carol, ever the apprentice to parry with the Nagual, piped up early.

"I noticed rental vans aren't supposed to be driven past the gift shop," she declared. She wasn't speaking to anyone in particular, and no one in particular responded.

Finally, Liz motioned to the Nagual. Liz didn't speak up often in the group although she came to the meetings regularly. It had taken me some time to realize that Liz was the Nagual's partner, but it didn't take me any time to realize that Liz and the Nagual were often at odds with each other. Liz's contribution to the group was as cook for all outings, accountant, truck driver, and general manager to the Nagual. I say "general manager" tongue-in-cheek, although from observation the Nagual depended on Liz for most things apart from her lectures on Tuesday and Thursday evenings. As she motioned to the left, off the narrow asphalt road, we saw a parking area that we'd nearly missed.

The heavy fog was dense, what I imagine it would be like to be in the midst of a metal-gray storm cloud. It was cold! So cold I was thankful for the down jacket Carla had mailed me the previous week from New York. Together with two pairs of gloves on my hands and a scarf wrapped like a turban around my head and neck, I still gasped at the cold when I stepped out of the van. As we crossed the road, Liz whispered in my ear, "Watch the Nagual, she's already loopy." I smiled. I liked loopy.

Every thirty or forty feet we paused and built a small pile of volcanic stones, on which we placed an M&M for a trail in case we found that we were lost on the return trip. The volcanic stones were easy to find: we were trudging along a hillside with no vegetation, only stones, rocks and boulders of black and purple hue, colors characteristic of volcanic emission.

"Hey, do you think the Nagual knows where the lake is?" Carol asked Suzanne, both of them trudging along behind me. I couldn't see either one of them in the fog, but their voices traveled clearly.

"Without the fog it would be easy. We'll see how she finds her way this time." Suzanne was referring to the retreat last year when there'd been no fog and no freezing temperatures. Comparisons between the two retreats had already been circling amongst the older apprentices.

"Well, I don't think it was the best decision to come in this weather but the Nagual ignored me when I suggested we go someplace else." Carol didn't hold back her opinion, although Suzanne didn't respond. After trudging along slowly in the fog for forty minutes with a trail of M&M towers behind us, the Nagual called a halt. Once the crunch, crunch of everyone's boots had ceased on the volcanic slope the sound of a not-too-distant car could be easily heard.

The Nagual instructed Barbara to go ahead of the group at a ninety-degree left turn. Barbara began to ascend the mountain alone, looking for the path to the lake. Slowly she disappeared in the fog as the rest of us milled around waiting for directions from the Nagual. The Nagual used the opportunity for a teaching.

"What are you telling yourself about not reaching the lake? What was your intent when we started out? Feel the energy in the fog. What is the fog saying to you?" Asking us to focus on the moment at hand helped to dispel some of the grumblings the Nagual must have heard as easily as I had heard them as we hiked along. It was a moment to be accountable, as a group member, for one's behavior and language.

Barb spoke up. "I sense we need to head back in that direction," and she pointed back and left from where we stood. The Nagual called out for Barbara to return and the group turned to retrace our steps. The fog continued to obscure anything farther than a foot in front of our faces.

Twenty minutes into the return trip, we came upon a large outcropping of rock. The Nagual announced to the group that we would do "Toltec flying." I volunteered to go first, and she directed me to stand on the edge of the rock ledge. I wasn't sure how high the rock ledge was from the ground since the fog continued to be heavy, and blanketed our view. Two people grasped my hands after I extended them behind me and I leaned forward over the ledge. The Nagual then directed me to intone the sound "Om," a word the Himalayan sages vocalized repeatedly, like a chant, to create inner clarity. As I began to tone

Om, I relaxed into the forward lean, lifting my voice as loudly as I could. The coldness disappeared and I had the sensation of lifting off the ground.

Four additional people flew in like manner. Suddenly, the fog lifted. One minute we could barely see two feet ahead, and the next minute our surroundings had become clear. The rock ledge we were flying from was fifteen feet or so above the ground. The path we'd carved along the slope parallel to the road by thirty feet could be seen clearly. We saw the insignificant distance we'd hiked relative to the size of the mountain. Then, miraculously, the sun broke through the gray sky! Instantly, the temperature rose and warmed our cheeks as though we were standing before a crackling fire.

"Someone needed to pay attention to my comments when we first hiked by this rock outcropping," the Nagual declared, as people pondered whether the Toltec flying or the Nagual herself had been the cause of the disappearance of the fog. "Maybe by doing so we could have lifted the mist much earlier," she continued.

"You were waiting for us to help direct you?" I asked incredulously.

"When I'm deep into second attention, I need someone to attend to my offhanded comments. It helps me to hear myself," she explained.

Second attention is a vast domain of awareness that goes unnoticed by most people. First attention is everything we see, feel, and think on a daily basis, whereas second attention is the flip side – everything that's happening in the Universe that we don't see or aren't aware of. The Toltec apprentice strove to go into the second attention as a means of increasing awareness.

Over the next forty minutes we hiked in the opposite direction and just over the crest on a barely visible volcanic path, until we laid eyes on the lake. It was stunning: a small reservoir internally fed by underground melt year round. With no greenery to speak of except for the algae that glowed an eerie green on the edges of the ice-cold water, the lake rippled with a mystical wind. The wind blew across the iron-red and ashen-gray volcanic rock, circumscribing it in every direction, hitting the lake like hundreds of soft reverberations of unspoken sound.

I felt expansive and without a care in the world, as altered in perception as I'd ever been on hallucinogenic plants or on the massage table. Life was glorious, fulfilling, and beautiful. The altitude contributed to the feeling of awe, but not everyone responded in the same manner. Some felt nauseous and some felt exhausted.

The Nagual held a ceremony at the edge of the lake. She called each one of us to her and handed us a stone. With a tone of reverence, she said to me, "The Lady of the Lake welcomes you. She says to acknowledge who you are and stand firm within yourself. She says your heart is open. Trust." In the palm of her hand was a stone that had been cut in half. The milky white crystals inside the stone mingled with the blood red of the stone. In that moment, the stone was my heart, open, diamond-cut crystals bathed in rich red, pulsing with energy.

I reached for the Nagual and hugged her with gratitude. The serenity and energy of the lake swirled around us. I stepped aside as the Nagual spoke to each person in turn.

As we left the lake, I fell into place behind the Nagual. A feeling of bliss permeated me. The air was light, the sun was shining, and I didn't have a care in the world. As I followed in her footsteps, I was silent and maintained a quiet mind. To the best of my ability, I placed my feet immediately in the footprints of the Nagual's. She was literally one step ahead of me. Not only did I not speak to anyone, internally my mind was silent. This was a first for me: to maintain a silent mind amidst a group of people in an unfamiliar environment. Later I came to know that unknown locations were excellent conduits for silencing the chatter of the mind, just as yoga, meditation, or listening to a binaural tape aided in accomplishing the same goal. I was familiar with those ways of entering silence, but following in a Nagual's footsteps on holy ground was new to me.

Suddenly I stumbled. Odd. We were walking on even ground and the path was clear of rocks and boulders. I was stepping precisely into the footsteps of the Nagual as she walked, and she hadn't lost her footing or taken a misstep. I tracked my immediate thought. In a mind that had been empty just a moment before, it wasn't difficult to grab the single thought: *You had wanted to leave a gesture of gratitude for the Lady of the Lake, and you forgot to do it.*

I picked up my pace. The Nagual was walking fast; her lead ahead of the group was now a hundred feet or more. Several group members were experiencing fatigue due to the high altitude, and they labored slowly behind us while the Nagual and I continued far ahead of them.

And then a second stumble and a second errant thought: *I am being greedy by following the Nagual so closely while everyone else follows at a distance.* Two criticisms leveled against myself, and the instantaneous result was to lose my pace and stumble. The mind and body connection was crystal clear because my mind had been wiped clean of any thought. Those two thoughts had stood in an ocean of void; and like beams from a lighthouse on the cliffside, they were easily recognized. I hurried to step alongside the Nagual and told her what had happened.

"Yes, many people recognize the benefit of following me as I tap into the energy lines of the earth."

I wanted her to say more, although I thought I knew what she meant. The reason I loved hiking the Modjeska Grade in my backyard in Southern California was because I had done the same thing without giving it a name. I had hiked those trails weekly for three years, without thinking about what was happening; nevertheless, the feelings of openness, of euphoria, of utter contentment and well-being matched what I was feeling as I followed the Nagual. My body knew what was happening and continued to call me back to that mountain trail over and over. Here on the slopes of the volcano, I connected to that feeling once again.

Returning to a silent mind, I heard the voices of the lava rocks. They were calling out to me. When the stones would call to me while hiking the Modjeska Grade, I'd pick the stones up and take them home with me, but the Nagual had warned about picking up stones or artifacts while we were "out and about." The objects were part of the land, and the land that made up Mauna Kea was holy to the Hawaiian people. We were to respect their request that nothing be taken from the volcano.

"The stones are calling out to me," I panted as I tried to keep up with the Nagual's pace.

"This is a mysterious place," the Nagual answered, "and you are responding to the energy you feel from the land." As she walked ahead, I paused at a large outcropping of stone. I spoke aloud from my heart and kissed the rock in gratitude for reaching out to me. My tears dropped softly on the volcanic stone of Mauna Kea, sacred mountain to the Hawaiians that was so willing to communicate to a human being.

March 18

Seated in front of the television, the entire group was watching the movie *A.I. Artificial Intelligence*.[4] The movie presented a philosophical conundrum involving a "mecha," or robot of the future, that was created with the capacity to experience love, and yet found the experience to be filled with unexpected pathos and pain. It was a tale of morality, deeply affecting and full of anguish.

Sam stepped outside the sliding glass door and walked around the corner of the house. Sam and his girlfriend, Tina, had come from their home state of New Hampshire for the weekend retreat. He was the only guy attending the retreat, and the couple comprised the only newcomers in attendance distinct from our Tuesday/Thursday group. Sam appeared friendly, although he would primarily interact only with the Nagual or his girlfriend. That way of interacting certainly rang a familiar bell with me. After stepping outside he returned a few minutes later, slipping his small pipe back into this pocket as he entered the living room. The sweet, sticky smell of marijuana clung to him as he settled into his chair.

Throughout the previous weekend he'd smoked often, gauging by the number of times he'd slipped away from the group, and upon his return the distinctive odor clung to his clothing like an aura. When he returned this time, he put his arm around his girlfriend and turned his attention to the television.

As I continued watching the movie, I grew uneasy at the plot, which was about the creation of a robot with human feelings. Was this an ethical thing for mankind to do? Top it off with the fact that the robot was a young child who was then abandoned by his human parents and I was doubly disturbed. The movie was bleak. Sam pulled himself out of his armchair and once again slid out of the room. Back in five minutes, he brought with him the distinct smell of weed once again.

The movie continued. Violence erupted as the community of robots began to be used for human entertainment in a circus setting where they battled each other to utter destruction. Sam let himself out the door for the third time. "What in the hell is he doing?" I asked, seething, as I watched him go. "Can't he go fifteen minutes without smoking?" All day he had removed himself from the group at consistent intervals, always returning just as the pipe slid from his hand into the hollow of his pocket.

Check yourself, Jess, I cautioned myself. *You're no stranger to smoking weed; where is your judgment coming from? Let the man be without your negative thoughts,* I chided myself.

Sam returned. I heard the glass panel move along the slider as he pushed the patio door closed. His actions were quiet and unobtrusive. Conversely, my reaction was judgmental.

"Byron Katie" that thought, I heard an internal voice say. Byron Katie had developed a process of investigation that she termed "The Work," specifically four questions that assist in determining the underlying beliefs that hinder a person from accepting their reality.[5] Her proposition states that all of what one says about others is projection, particularly when what is said is accompanied by intense feeling. If we observe ourselves closely, we can see that our opinions and beliefs about others are disowned opinions and beliefs about ourselves. If taken to heart, applying this assertion of Byron Katie's will change your world and turn it upside down.

After familiarizing myself with "The Work," rather than going through the whole process of writing out the four questions as she suggested, I got to the point where I could simply say to myself, *Byron Katie that thought,* and then turn the projection back onto myself. Those thoughts and opinions that were the most judgmental were decidedly the strongest projections.

In this case, the tirade of my judgments went something like this: "He is so damn reliant on smoking that weed. All day he has excused himself to go and smoke. That weed has got him in a vise grip; he's addicted to it. I didn't smoke. However, what was the weed symbolic of in my life?" Like an arrow flying directly toward a red bull's-eye, I got the connection, and my *cohesion*, my perceptual awareness, shifted powerfully.

As often as Sam smoked his weed, I used *ideas*, and just as addictively. I saw my heavy judgment projected onto Sam. I relied on ideas to do for me what I suspected weed did for Sam – and doing so was not okay with me. It was not the weed nor the ideas that were "wrong," but the fact that I held the high moral ground that determined the action in and of itself to be wrong. "Idealism" had become an arbiter of my thinking, and dictated too many of my actions.

Suddenly, the visual world around me – a dozen people seated in front of a television screen watching a movie – evaporated, and a blank screen was before my eyes. I was paralyzed; my body had turned to stone. Simultaneously, energy swept through the vessel that was my body like a bonfire exploding through a narrow tunnel. The heat was unbearable! The part of me that held onto perception, or the *assemblage point*, seemed to tumble all over the room bouncing off the furniture, the walls, the people, as though it was no longer held within the confines of my skin.

The assemblage point is the mechanism inside each person that houses the location of our perception, whereas perception itself is the mechanism inside each person that determines *what* we pay attention to. An analogy for the assemblage point would be the computer chip inside a cell phone that allows the phone its functionality, whereas the keyboard would be our perception or the combination of numerals we use to dial specific people. When someone uses their cell phone they don't give a lot of thought to the computer chip that makes the phone work but they know to input the numerals to dial the people they want to speak with.

The analogy breaks down though because the computer chip inside a cell phone doesn't move around in its casing, whereas the computer chip belonging to each person, or the assemblage point, can and does move around. When it moves, it allows the person to see, hear, feel, and know things that they've previously been unaware of. This movement of the assemblage point occurs both accidentally and purposefully.

Shamans have known for centuries how to move their assemblage point as a means of practicing divination, healing, and sorcery. Most people's assemblage point gets moved every night when they have dreams, although most people don't know how it happens and know even less that they can cause it to happen in a purposeful way. This movement of the assemblage point can cause unusual physical reactions, which is what happened to me.

Dizzy and nauseous, I glanced down to see whether or not my body was still seated on the chair and my eyes were working properly. Yep, the "I" that was my body was still seated in the chair.

I turned my head in the Nagual's direction, hoping I could locate her in the room. Surely she was able to sense the energy vortex that had replaced the "me" seated in my chair a moment before, but her eyes were glued to the screen. She didn't look in my direction, and I realized that I expected her to sense what was happening from an energetic stance amongst her apprentices. She didn't acknowledge my upheaval, though, as it continued.

Now my mind was a projectile traveling away from me at a speed greater than light. It was no longer inside my head. There was no internal dialogue. Nothing. Instead, there was the void, and this void was immense. I recognized the infinite size of it. For a split second, I lunged toward insanity. That would be the easy route, to lose my marbles in a split second, never to recover. My entire mind was gone already, so why not?

I heard the words in my head, *Silent knowledge will protect you*, although I didn't know what that could possibly mean. I knew silent knowledge was inner knowing, gained apart from the operation of the mind, but how could it protect me?

"Hold on, don't panic," the voice chuckled, explaining what had happened. "The assemblage point has shifted further than you're accustomed to. How solidly your judgment keeps it fixed! And then to have your mind dethroned at the same instance…"

Whomever that voice belonged to, and I believed it to be my higher self distinct from my mind, it was not in the least alarmed or concerned as it assisted me in that near-drop-into-insanity moment. Slowly, I followed its lead and gained equilibrium. Having knowledge about what was happening protected me from "losing my marbles" or losing my total grip on reality. Yes! The movement of the assemblage point had the potential to be significant indeed!

All of the parts of me that had been blasted into space (figuratively speaking) slowly coalesced. My hearing returned. My mind returned. As soon as it lodged itself back into place, I could feel the heaviness with which my mind operated. Slowly, slowly, my mind was beginning to do what it thinks it does best: think. It was already reflecting on its near suicide. I shifted in the chair to reassure myself that my body was no longer paralyzed.

The dialogue that continued in the movie was now within earshot. As the movie played to the end, I continued to observe my reactions. I was surprised at the freedom I felt. No longer was I opposed to the ethical dilemma in the movie. No longer did I notice Sam coming or going. One of the primary goals for moving the assemblage point had occurred: my usual manner of looking at the world had changed. What a relief to no longer feel my previous judgment toward Sam!

As the credits began to roll, I approached the Nagual. I told her what had happened. "In time those experiences will come closer and closer together and you'll be able to hold onto them for longer and longer periods," she said.

"I felt like I was going to lose my mind," I confessed.

"Losing the mind is a good thing," she said, smiling and giving me a reassuring hug.

Lying in bed that evening, I went over the experience again and again. Freeing oneself from the identification with the mind is a freedom human beings seldom attain. It is what meditation is about, what yoga is about, and what students on many spiritual paths seek. Experiencing the stopping of the internal chatter that is the mind allowed me to experience a state of non-duality. In that non-duality, I was free from my limiting beliefs on Sam's behavior and free from my own limiting beliefs on ideas. It was a desirable state to be in! Being seated in the North continued to challenge me in regards to those beliefs that kept me tethered to inflexible ways of viewing the world.

April 6, Daytime

The wave spilled into the kayak, soaking my shorts with warm seawater. For the weekend, the winds were going to be "Kona" explained the Nagual seated behind me in the two-man kayak. She likened them to "Santa Ana" winds in California, seasonal winds that are warmer-than-usual air currents that get all in a bother for a couple of days, and then calm themselves as though exhausted after a workout at the gym. I had a feeling of expansive freedom as though I mirrored the feisty winds. Our destination was Chinaman's Hat, an island dollop off the coast of Oahu that the Hawaiians held in high revere. The energy emanating from this small volcanic button was legendary for causing strange behavior to those who came near.

Several other kayaks were behind us, paddling furiously in the wild winds. I concentrated on my hand positions, the depth and height of my paddles, and the coordination of pulling the paddles through the water at a rhythm and angle that would cause the kayak to glide smoothly just as the Nagual had instructed.

She had assigned people to kayaks and I was pleasantly surprised to be paired with her. I was conscious of my performance after Carol had made a comment in the car on the drive over: "Well, I sure don't want to be paired with someone who's never paddled before. It means I'm doing all the work." At one point, halfway to our destination, I turned around to see what the Nagual was up to when I didn't hear her paddles dipping into the water. "Hey, you're not paddling," I jested.

"No, you're doing just fine in the lead position," she laughed.

The day was one of those days in Hawaii that give credence to its reputation as one of the most highly-sought vacation spots in the world. The sky had high, wispy clouds above the Kona wind currents, the ocean waves were at peace with the land (although surfers might describe the waves very differently – as in "white capped," making them useless for surfing), and we had all the time in the world to dally in nature.

I soon discovered that it wasn't necessary to turn my head to either side as I dipped the paddle into the water again and again. In fact, the rhythm became smoother and the work less strenuous as I faced forward. The kayak sliced smoothly through the water. My "body, mind, heart, attention, and interest"[6] were all in one place. No better description could be found for an expansive, non-dual, enlightened moment.

The transcendent feeling I'd had while hiking the volcano was present. "I can attach to the energy lines of the earth here in the water!" I expressed, surprised. Even though I didn't turn around, I could feel the Nagual smile. Because I was drawn to the earth rather than to the water, the experience of being united with the ocean was a mystery; but here I was, feeling the wonder of being immersed in one of the most elemental sources on the planet.

As all four of the kayaks reached the narrow channel leading to the beach, the paddlers waited for the lull between swells to push forward onto the tiny shore. We pulled the kayaks onto the sand and jumped out. To our left was a lava overhang. Underneath the bleached volcanic overhang, the ocean tides had leached out a small enclosure. When the tide was low, the enclosure permitted four or five people to crawl inside as long as they drew up their knees tightly for seating once they wiggled into the small cave. The tide was high enough to gush inside and soak the lower half of our bodies as we waited for the Nagual to commence her teaching. She perched atop another lava outcrop that formed part of the outside wall of the tiny, natural womb.

"How's everyone feeling?" The Nagual did a check in. It was quiet for a moment as though no one wanted to admit not feeling gloriously fine on such a perfect day. Unexpectedly on the paddle over, she had turned to her left and announced, "Death is present." In the near distance a buoy bobbed up and down keeping time with the ocean swells, and the Nagual had looked at the buoy as though it were a power to be reckoned with.

"I haven't seen it for some time, but there it is," and she nodded her head at the red and white object a short distance from us. I stared at the buoy, trying to perceive a difference in the energy from moments before when the day was a picture perfect postcard to now when Death was being perceived as floating on the horizon. I had wanted the Nagual to say more about the presence of Death but she said no more.

Linda had spoken softly in the kayak next to us. "I feel spooky for some reason. I don't want to feel fearful, but this is a challenge for me to come here. I have lived my entire life on this island, but I've never ventured on this side." A new member to the group, she was eager to learn how to read energy and how to tell the difference between internal versus external energy. I shared her eagerness.

"How about everyone else?" The Nagual encouraged more responses.

"The paddle over was great, but now I feel very small sitting here," I ventured. I couldn't determine the origin of my feelings. The Nagual's comment about Death had been odd, and neither had she explained her comment. Was her lack of clarity influencing my feelings now? Or had I too easily merged with the feelings expressed by Linda? The Nagual had a favorite phrase: "There is no out there." Simple. But not simple. A koan that was difficult to grasp. "Out there" was a projection of what was inside. It was Byron Katie in a different syntax.

"Death is out there," spoke the Nagual to all of us squeezed into the small cave. "See that buoy, about a quarter mile out?" The Nagual pointed over her left shoulder. "That's the same buoy we passed on our way here. You are feeling its presence. Now, I want to do energy work with each one of you here. Linda, you stay first. The rest of you wait outside. I will call you when it's your turn."

I had no idea what the Nagual meant when she said, "You are feeling Death's presence." And neither did I have any idea what she meant by "doing energy work with each one of us here." The Nagual hadn't indicated what she meant, and I wasn't going to ask for clarification. I'd learned while working with Bruce, the massage therapist, that our bodies hold energy, and that energy does only one of two things: it either increases our sense of well-being or it blocks and depletes our energy, so I assumed that the Nagual was going to work at increasing our energy. And I'd learned from the Nagual that experience often trumped words, so I assumed again that her work would have the desired impact on me whether or not I knew what she was doing. Eventually, whatever she did energetically would translate into words. It was frustrating not to be told ahead of time what "doing energy work" meant and what Death might be up to, but I firmly believed that "actions" spoke louder than words, and that eventually my mind would catch up to what was happening to my body. I trusted that the Nagual knew what she was doing despite my frustration at her lack of explanation.

Crawling out of the cave, we left Linda and the Nagual and walked along the small shoreline. The spooky feelings from the cave evaporated, and I felt free and expansive again. When the Nagual called my name half an hour later, I returned and crawled into the small enclosure. The Nagual put her hand on my sternum and supported my back with her other hand. The usual feeling of heat and tiny bubbles exploded at the spot where her hand touched my chest.

"Be aware of a shift in your energy," she spoke suddenly. My eyes flew open and I looked at her. Her tone of voice had a sense of foreboding.

"I've shifted your energy the other direction."

"What direction?" I blurted out.

"Counterclockwise" answered the Nagual.

"What did you do that for?" The question had more force

than I intended. The force came not from the demand to know why, but because I'd asked a question, although that wasn't clear in the asking.

"I don't know. It just seemed to be the thing to do," the Nagual answered evenly, with no undue reaction to my pressing question. At the moment she said, "I don't know," I had an epiphany, much like Robert Monroe's rote in which there is a download of information previously unknown. The knowledge that came to me felt big because I'd not conceived of it before.

My moment of clarity had to do with expectations, expectations on a teacher, expectations for teachings that would "Wow!" and expectations for an outing such as the day had promised. I wanted this Nagual to articulate in a manner I could grasp each and every time I spoke with her; I wanted each and every one of her teachings to deliver a golden nugget of truth; I wanted every outing to be "out of this world." In the same moment this epiphany hit, I also realized that I wasn't unusual in this desire. The placement of responsibility for my life onto the Nagual was the "student" position, or so many followers assumed, but this very mindset prevented the student from stepping into his or her own Power. The proverbial lightbulb hanging over my head had turned on.

I stared at the Nagual as the epiphany unfolded in a matter of seconds. She turned and indicated for everyone to man the kayaks for the return trip home.

Settling into the energy lines of the earth, I paddled with ease. The euphoria I had felt on the trip to the tiny island returned in equal measure, and within no time we were back at the parking lot. Several of the women commented on the wind change and how difficult it had been for them to paddle against it. They attributed the wind change to the Nagual, saying that in the past she had been known to reverse its direction. Standing next to the Nagual, I whispered, "I thought the trip back was effortless, really." She smiled.

"That is what we made of our experience, whereas they made something else of it." Her comment struck me as profound. For a brief moment I grasped her koan, "There is no out there." Internal and external were simply a reflection of each other. If I could learn to recognize that my surroundings were a mirror of my inner being, I'd go a long way in decreasing the sense of duality that so often plagued me – and not me alone. The duality that most of mankind experiences keeps us from ever moving into an experience of oneness with all that is available to us. What a challenge to bring myself into a state of being in which the freedom of each moment is my birthright!

April 6, Evening

For three months I had given the Nagual a massage once a week, as was our agreement. When I had worked at a spa doing massage all day, the majority of clients wanted a good, overall, invigorating massage that eased surface tension from their limbs, neck, face, and shoulders; in effect, the major portion of the superficial fascia. However, there are many forms of massage, there are many types of massage therapists, and there are many types of bodies to be massaged. A good match was made when the massage therapist and the person being massaged wanted what each had to offer.

When Bruce and I had worked together, we'd wanted to explore anywhere in the body that our hands might be drawn to, a focus that made the feel-good massage a secondary gain. That "feel good" portion of the massage was the proverbial cherry on top of the sundae.

We'd mapped energy in the body and explored the muscles and fascia as they were a schema for the chi that we could feel through our fingertips. This chi was our life force. As we worked on the body, we listened to the chi as though it carried on a dialogue with us. To work in this way was a match made in heaven, whereas I felt that the superficial, "feel good" massage was assembly-line work.

In addition, a massage therapist can often feel whether or not their client has had previous massage. They can feel a kinesthetic quality in the body that announces the client's massage experience through their hands. The Nagual had this feel; I knew she enjoyed massage.

On the evening after our return from the kayak trip to Chinaman's Hat, the energy of that place had remained with us. To ride on that energy felt like a high, a natural euphoria that lifted us into a state of Samadhi, a state of oneness between the mind, consciousness, the observer and the observed. The feeling was one of ease, contentment, and no thought. The late afternoon light permeated the room as though it were partner to our state of being. The faint odor of sea salt wafted off my arms as I poured oil into my hands. The Nagual's dogs and cats were settled, and we had the evening to work.

After light, warm-up strokes over the Nagual's body, I settled in on a massage technique called "unwinding," a slow motion that inherently induces a state of calm. It is also used to release stuck energy. I took one of the Nagual's legs in my hands and lifted it off the massage table five inches or so. The Nagual had already told me she had chronic discomfort in one of her hips, and this was the leg attached to that problematic hip. While holding it in this position, I tuned in to the rhythm of the leg and moved it accordingly.

Unwinding is a technique associated with cranial unwinding, in which the head is held in the masseuse's hands and slowly moved to the rhythm of the cranial-sacral fluid. At each pause in that rhythm, or stop in the movement, however minute, I let the stuck energy of that moment free itself, as I held the leg perfectly still. It is slow, etheric work. It tunes the therapist and the client into infinitesimal movements within the client's body that hold body memories. It opens the window to a kinesthetic and symbolic microscopic view of body knowledge. As I worked, there was little conversation between us.

At the level of in-depth work generated by the unwinding, any conversation between the client and the masseuse feels ponderous and slow, and the normal volume of conversation sounds too loud. I valued the silence in the room.

There was much to explore in the Nagual's hip. It was loaded with history, with images that popped into my head as I worked, which helped me to decipher what my hands were feeling. The images are not always welcomed, but it is for the client to do what they will with their massage experience, not for the massage therapist to impose upon them the images they see. The remainder of the Nagual's body was quiet energetically, except for her hands. In that moment in time, her hands held all of the energetic "electricity" or chi in her body.

Her stomach was quiet – unexplored would be another way to describe it. Not too unusual. The stomach is an intimate organ, and it is commonly virgin territory in massage. Most spa rules prohibit stomach work altogether. But for me, the stomach was a gold mine; many are the mysteries to be explored in that muscular organ.

I wondered how in touch the Nagual was with her body. I had invited her into the mystery of the energy within the body, whether flowing or stuck, that I felt when I worked. This intimate work between the one lying on the table and the one leaning over the table is a relationship. The relationship deepens when it takes place on a weekly basis. The Nagual had the ability to be a conduit for energy. I had seen and felt it up close. But she did not know her body. I, on the other hand, could not look across the ocean swells and see Death in a buoy. My hope was that we could learn from each other.

April 21

I finally had a root canal on my bottom, left molar, the tooth that had given me such persistent pain my first week in Hawaii. It had been seven months since I'd healed the molar. "You'll know it's healed when you can eat without pain on both sides of your mouth," the voice had informed me during a meditation. Since that time, I had eaten without any indication that the tooth had ever been sore, throbbing, or pounding inside my head during that first week at the YMCA. The pain from the tooth during that first week of living in Hawaii had been forgotten. Then suddenly it had returned, and I noticed that my left jaw was puffy. As I massaged it, I could feel the soreness inside my cheek.

In the interim six months, plenty had happened regarding my understanding of healing. Two ideas had shifted in my awareness. One was an idea I'd brought with me when I came to study with the Nagual (amongst a million, if truth be known), and the second idea had been introduced by the Nagual. When the two had come together, a newly emerged concept of healing had fallen into place. Here's how it went:

The year before my move to Hawaii, I had plunged into a wild, exhilarating love affair. It was the first time since my marriage had ended that such feelings had erupted. I had thought them long gone since the divorce. Such powerful, raw feeling! The relationship with Steve hadn't lasted long; but in its short life span, it had set loose a rollercoaster of feelings. But then, as the relationship had careened to a stop, I had been catapulted into a state of despair during a massage session with Bruce. As he worked on me, I had gone into the void. Time and space had literally disappeared. The experience had felt as though the quality in the void was pure potential, and that anything and everything was possible while in that state.

Generally speaking, human beings are filled to the brim with ideas, values, socialization, ego, beliefs, et cetera. All of these things were the filter systems the Nagual had taught us about months ago. The void gets pushed out of our awareness and, hence, out of existence. But as Bruce had worked on me, all of those perceptive lenses had dropped away and "Bam!" there I'd been. Silent knowledge (that voice that speaks apart from the mind) had been fully present. "With or without Steve" was the same. For one earth-shattering moment, I had known that whether or not the relationship continued was of equal significance, neither one being better nor worse than the other. I'd had total, complete, irreversible freedom, without value, judgments, morals, or emotions with which to view the outcome.

Eventually, the relationship with Steve had come to an end, and thereafter the phrase became, "With or without is the same." In the same way that I used "Byron-Katie-that-thought" to sift through projections, I used the mantra, "With or without is the same" when an attachment circumvented my well-being. The two koans helped me to dislodge belief systems that felt binding.

The Nagual taught that there was no right or wrong, only differences in preference. But human beings attach value to their opinions, in effect making them inviolable to anyone else. I had played out this scenario with Sam during our recent excursion to the Big Island. The Nagual often used emotions as an example of value: some people expressed anger to the exclusion of sadness; some people primarily expressed worry; some people showed only guilt. From a full palate of available emotions, people will consistently and doggedly use only one or two avenues of expression. It's not that their choice is wrong or right, limiting or unlimited, better or worse; instead it's, simply and profoundly, *different*.

This manner of viewing the world – that there exists only differences rather than absolutes – carries all the way through to differences between Eastern and Western medicine, differences between energetic and conventional medical healing, differences between our full range of emotions, even differences between wanting vanilla or chocolate ice cream.

As long as I am mindful of Intent, as long as I'm not scattering my energies to the four corners of the earth, and as long as I'm in the moment rather than projecting into the past or the future, the state of being is the same. Thus taught the Nagual: "With or without is the same."

By the time the molar began to cause swelling and inflammation in my cheek, I had put the two concepts together related to healing. Now I wanted healing to occur regardless of the manner in which it took place, a very different place to be in from when I had expected to heal the tooth myself seven months ago.

When I first arrived on the island, I had operated from the belief that I should heal whatever was ailing my body because I had healing abilities. It was my responsibility, therefore something I "should" do. Sounds ugly when I write it down on paper. I had twisted all up in a wad the gift of healing with the burden of healing. My definition of healing excluded a Western medical model as an inferior one. I had canonized my preference for healing by becoming attached to only one choice.

Finally I could see that healing takes place through any number of venues, that healing is specific to the occasion in which it takes place, and that differences do not determine moral deliberations. The healing of my tooth had become a multidimensional affair; exactly as the Nagual had suggested the first time I'd met her.

Part Three: East

– The direction of new beginnings, of the sunrise, of new life. It is the direction that promotes movement from personal mythology to visionary sight. East is the place of becoming a co-creator with the Universe in our daily lives.

East is seeing with the eyes of the heart from the center of our soul.

May 2

At the end of each Tuesday and Thursday meeting, members in the group would share a hug with each other. As greetings and farewells go, a hug is one of the best exchanges shared between people. On this night, after walking around and hugging half the people in the room, I found myself standing in front of Barb with the intention of a "goodnight" hug.

I was mindful that a month ago, during the weekend trip to the Big Island, Barb and I had had an awkward exchange. Later, as we'd hiked up the path to the volcanic lake located halfway up the slope of Mauna Kea, we'd made amends. It had been a mutual exchange, and I believed the rift between us had been repaired. Since that time, whenever I'd hugged Barb, the feeling had been of utter calm and stillness.

No one else in the group gave hugs with the tranquility that Barb did. Her hug felt like that of a mother who held her infant in her arms – no tension and total acceptance. I reached for Barb and she reached for me. The hug was warm and not hurried in any way; but tonight something was different.

"I don't know what has happened," Barb commented, "but when I hug you I feel something right here." She placed her fingers on her chest at the level of her heart. Her comment reminded me of the saying, "Have a nice day." It had as much – or as little – definition as it could possibly have. As she spoke, I recalled her having made the same comment earlier in the week, as we'd shared our first hug after our weekend trip. I had felt like I was bundled up before a cozy fire. The hug had felt genuine and Barb's comment had no accompanying agenda that I could tell. This time, however, the same comment seemed to have something attached to it and Barb was not smiling.

"What do you feel?" I asked, perplexed.

"I feel pressure," Barb replied, gesturing to her neck. "As

though something is stuck right here, and it can't quite make it up through my throat."

"So it feels uncomfortable?" I probed.

Barb nodded her head in agreement and couldn't seem to share more than that. I felt stuck along with Barb. I didn't know if she was uncomfortable hugging me because of our disagreement a month ago, or if she had food lodged in her throat from dinner. She was not going to give me any other emotional clue beyond "stuck," although I could clearly see that she was uneasy, so I ventured to share my own experience.

"For me the hug was warm and accepting; I didn't feel any tension. Looks like your experience is very different from mine."

The hug had been a shared action, resulting in two vastly different experiences. I was reminded of the paddle home from the seashore cave and how others in the group experienced the ocean conditions as difficult and laborious, whereas the Nagual and I had experienced it with a feeling of joy. I was reminded of the Nagual's koan, "There is no out there."

How did "difference" relate to "sameness," and where did they fit in a world in which external and internal were illusory anyway? I wondered whether "sameness" and "difference" were not two ends of a continuum and the middle position, the position of neutrality, was the location to strive for.

The Nagual's teaching on the koan, "There is no out there," came to mind again. Consistently, over the past few months, I had observed the events happening around me as though a mirror into my soul, which is how the Nagual defined the koan. When non-duality was present in my inner life, it was evidenced in my external surroundings, and there would be an experience of alignment between my outer and inner worlds. Whenever my experience was one of duality, the same mirror would be present but events would arise that would inform me of my inner disequilibrium. For example, what was happening in the group with the Nagual would be reflected in my job at the agency.

Just the day before, I had been seated at the office with Marianne. She had been talking about Megan, one of the young case managers.

"Megan is always going on and on about how difficult life is and her boyfriend Jeff is blah, blah, blah…" Marianne had intoned. Her view of Megan was that she was burdened with her own life, and that the chalice of life was already half-empty at a mere twenty-three years of age.

I had sat across the desk from Marianne, observing her body language. Her arms had been crossed over each other, with each hand holding the elbow of the opposite arm. She had been trying to keep herself warm despite wearing a sweater and light jacket. The temperature outside had been in the seventies, but the temperature in that small cubicle of an office had been ice-cold, with one too many air ducts converging directly over Marianne's desk. "Something to do with how they partitioned the office space," Marianne often explained. But my impression was that she was more than just physically cold; she often looked miserable and unhappy. At the time, I wondered whether or not Marianne was projecting onto Megan, and she was really the one who wanted to go on and on about how difficult her life was.

Both women, Barb and Marianne, had shared their burdens with me. One felt burdened while giving me a hug, and one had shared her story of being burdened with a colleague. If I was understanding the Nagual's lesson, "There is no out there," both of them were reflections of my world. Hmm, something was going on here for me to look at. If I connected their concerns as though they were my concerns, whom or what was *I* burdened with? The connection came quickly: my relationship with the Nagual.

I was beginning to see that I had been completely enamored with the Nagual. I had believed that she alone was going to answer my questions, enlarge the body of my knowledge, challenge my weaknesses, build upon my strengths, and guide me as I walked the Toltec path. After all, that was her job, right? Without her, I could go no further on this path. In fact, that's what she had said the first time I'd met her: "In order to be an apprentice on this path, you must study with a Nagual." That was the design of the relationship between Nagual and apprentice from millennia past, or so both of us had believed. It was the person of the Nagual that had the extra energy the apprentice needed. In order to advance as a Toltec, whether that be a sorcerer, a seer, or a "man of knowledge," one had to be under the tutelage of a Nagual. The apprentice was to be trained by a Nagual who had gone before them and so could map the way. How many books had I read that had begun with, "I apprenticed with..." as a prelude to the story? Without that ticket, there was no going to the attraction. I was beginning to challenge that assumption. But first, the Nagual had to come down from the lofty height where I'd placed her.

The "idea" of the Nagual and "the Nagual" were two very different people, and I was beginning to experience the Nagual for who she was rather than what I expected her to be. If truth be told, I didn't like her much, although I didn't like myself much for even thinking that. Not every teacher I'd had or doctor I'd gone to became a personal friend. I went to them to gain from their expertise, not to develop a friendship. The Nagual was beginning to come down from the pedestal where I'd placed her long before I arrived.

May 5

Lying in bed very early in the morning, I gazed up at the ceiling, soaking up the absolute stillness. No one else was awake. There was no movement inside the house or upstairs in the duplex above us. The moment was perfect. Consciously, I began to move my assemblage point. I'd never been able to do it on my own before. I knew it was possible because of my reading Carlos Castaneda, but I'd not done it before now. Moving the assemblage point can happen when we drink alcohol, when we ingest drugs, or when we "go crazy," such as being labeled schizophrenic. It rarely, if ever, happened volitionally or without an external impetus; that is unless we aimed for it to happen. Doing so was my aim on that morning as I lay in bed, wide-awake, with my body and mind completely still. My conscious Intent at that moment was for my assemblage point to move away from its accustomed position to a new one.

Suddenly, I am dreaming, and Cat appears at the foot of the bed, although I'm not seeing it with my eyes, because I lie on my stomach with my head turned to the left. I'd known for a long time that my consciousness could "see" without using the faculty of my eyes, so it is with absolute certainty that I know Cat is placing its paws on my top sheet. And, it is "the" Cat, with a capital C, because it has visited me before; however, always at its own behest rather than mine.

Slowly, with a purpose that is beyond the significance of daily reality (if it can be described in that way), Cat walks along the edge of the bed, placing each paw with precision and purpose. It has an appointment; it isn't here on a lark.

The weight of Cat is real, not more real than it had been in the past, but heavier than it had ever been. Cat is getting large.

Coming to the head of the bed, Cat prepares to lie down. Slowly, and with absolute deliberation, Cat begins to lower its body on top of my head. Simultaneously, I feel the weight and the whiskers and the greatness of Cat as it turns its head to look down at me. There is an absolute sense that Cat is aware of me in the room, and its actions are linked to my presence. Of course they are! I had bid Cat to come.

Whiskers tickle my cheek. The pungent, musky odor of Cat permeates my nostrils – never before have I smelled the odor of a wild cat. The odor is suffocating!

The temptation to open my eyes is tremendous. Too often in the past I have opened my physical eyes in order to gain confirmation that what I was "seeing" with my body was, in fact, real. *Don't do it!* I admonish myself. Gasping for a breath of air, I can feel panic coming on. Cat's weight is beginning to feel unbearable. The odor is thick and so musky as to take away completely what breath I have. I need fresh air!

I know it might seem odd that I could tell myself that my eyes were not a useful tool to see with, that my body had its own perceptive abilities, while also telling myself that I must have air to breathe or else I was going to suffocate. If the energy body can "see" without eyes, can't it breathe without air? Either my energy body didn't know its own capabilities (highly doubtful) or my physical body was clinging to its form and function (most likely). In that moment though, I couldn't decipher between the two.

Time passes differently in a state of heightened awareness. I'd heard how people involved in a car accident experience the accident in very distinct moments as though time is elongated, like a rubber band that gets stretched to the limits of its elasticity. Time doesn't operate in the same manner in which we're accustomed when we're not within the confines of time itself. That may sound obvious, but it's only when one is outside of the confines of time that one can see the limitations of being inside it.

When time is not an element of an experience, each moment of that experience takes on a distinct quality of permanence – as though it is the only element in our reality – because it is! In reality, there is nothing to compete with, compare to, or contrast against the moment we are in. There is only one moment, and that moment is now. That feeling of "Now" was what I had felt when Cat had first placed his paws on the edge of the bed; his movements had been purposeful and without an attachment to time.

As I absorb this insight, I move from wonder to intoxication. The Power of Cat mesmerizes me. Even though my physical body has the feeling of paralysis, I can also feel every cell of the billion cells encased inside my body as aware and alive. My mind shrinks to its intended size; it is as though a scale weighted with mind and body have finally been balanced, whereas before too much of the goods have been on the side of the mind.

Fear comes now. Slowly, I breathe air into my lungs in order to calm myself. I hear my own internal voice: *Fear is natural. Let it go. Don't let it overwhelm you.* Too often in the past, my fear has pulled me out of this "no-time" zone, too eager to return to what it knows. I work vigorously to sustain the experience rather than to let the fear pull me away, but gradually, groping and groaning with the effort, fear is gaining ground.

Again, I speak silently; this time, to Cat. "Thank you for coming! Don't let my fear drive you away! I want you here!" The imperatives are loud and clear, not in the least muffled for speaking them without the use of vocal cords. In this state of awareness, communication is telepathic.

A powerful, seductive thought suddenly occurs to me, and a desire stronger than I can hold back takes hold. The moment it comes to me I have to speak it aloud or else it will overwhelm me with an avalanche of longing. It will crush me with the weight of its largeness. Without hesitation and with total abandon and surrender of body, mind, and spirit, I say, "I will worship you forever!"

There is not a second more of ecstasy. Dread and remorse hit me equally, as has desire the second before. I rebound; a sacrificial lamb freeing itself from the altar. I am astounded at my offer!

"Worship" is a strong word to use and reminds me of giving my allegiance to God. I recoil at the thought of a heavenly being that religion tells me I owe my life to! And there is an act of surrender – surrender to a Cat! I have just given my life over to a Cat, an unearthly being! I have totally acquiesced to Power, a Power so alluring and seductive that I cannot refuse despite it being in feline form. The lavender stone had told me not to abandon myself to anything! What Power could cause me to capitulate so completely?

I have my wits about me enough to notice that Cat does not speak to me. But actions speak louder than words, at least in the world I am familiar with. I'm not so sure about the dreaming realm, but I suspect the deed of surrendering myself is a done deal regardless of how lightning fast I refute it in my mind. I am horrified at what I've done, and absolutely enamored at being in the Cat's presence.

Cat takes a pair of golden calipers, not the double-pronged instrument, but a three-pronged tool, and aims it at my head. A delicate instrument, I can see the glint from the metal as Cat begins to lower the calipers onto my head. Fear is rising as a throat full of bile, too quickly and with a sick taste. In every instance I have ever experienced of dreaming, of being in heightened awareness, or of an assemblage point shift, the feeling of fear is a signal that the experience is going to dissipate and disappear.

"Stay! Please! I want you here!" I plead. Perhaps if I call upon Cat, maybe he will help me stay in the experience for a longer period of time. I am determined to see this through for as long as I can possibly sustain my awareness. Slowly Cat lowers the calipers onto my head, carefully, like a medical instrument that needs exact measurement. And then my dreaming awareness begins to run out. The cohesion of my state begins to fade. Slowly Cat dissolves. The weight on my head lessens. The golden calipers disappear. The air clears of wild odor, and I come back to ordinary reality to find myself lying on my bed, my head turned to the left.

Back in my ordinary consciousness, I remained still as a statue in order to hold onto the experience for as long as I possibly could.

Ah! Cat represented Power! Never before had I put the two together. I hadn't known what I expected Power to be if it was to take physical form, but I hadn't expected it to be a wild cat. I was shaken. Who in the world offered their fealty to a cat? I was embarrassed. A cat!

It was early in the morning. My choices were two. Either I journeyed to consult with Castaneda in the cave or I called the Nagual.

I picked up the phone and dialed. The Nagual answered. Blurting out my story, I tried not to sound as desperate as I felt. I tried to convey how seductive Cat was. I tried to tell her how tantalizing, how tormenting it was to be in the presence of Cat. To have swooned with such a confession was as far from my experience as the core of the earth was from its surface – which is to say, unfathomably far.

I wanted the Nagual to explain my confusion over the concepts of "abandon" and "surrender," since I'd declared my devotion and obeisance to Cat in a manner that I'd not yet done with her or with my fellow apprentices. But my awareness of the significance of the experience had yet to dawn on me. It mattered little that I was embarrassed and uncertain of my actions. That, I was coming to see, was fear talking. The East was influencing the focal point of my Power by shifting it away from the Nagual and placing it within my own essence. I was beginning to claim my own Power rather than to surrender to another person or to another ideology as a replacement. Cat was me, and I was Cat;

and I was beginning to surrender to that realization.

The Nagual confirmed the nature of Power to entice beyond measure, to persuade beyond reason. The Nagual said that her teacher warned of two things: Power and old age. The Nagual said nothing about surrendering to Cat, but her last comment would take some unraveling. It was a rubric of Toltec wisdom: "Power is the core of who we are; there is no distinction."

May 8

For a few days after my time with Cat and the shift in assemblage point, I remained unsettled. The Nagual called it "reentry," akin to jetlag, during which time the world one is familiar with has yet to return to its normal cohesion. Sometimes, in that twilight nether world, my mind would take a back seat, while the wonder and mystery of silent knowledge would take the helm. All human beings experience a silent mind in small snippets, but they don't always know that this state of communion with the essence of all life is their birthright. This phenomenon belongs in the same category as our natural ability to be healers. These innate capabilities, or ways of being, are what healers, shamans, sorcerers, and even gurus, seek and realize.

The curious thing about this particular reentry period was that the uneasiness of this new silent knowledge was attaching itself to whatever my monkey mind tried to grasp. Round and round the monkey chased the weasel. Thinking about surrendering and acquiescing to Power *was* that monkey. I couldn't resolve for myself the Nagual's advice that I, "Surrender to this group," whom I viewed as lackluster in their commitment to the Toltec path, and the acquiescing instead to a Power inside me that showed itself as a wild animal. The debate was fast, furious, and cyclical, as well as solitary, because the Nagual wasn't interested in having such a discussion.

The Nagual defined the Toltec path as one of love and dominion. In her view, love was inclusive and unconditional, everyone was part of a greater whole regardless of endeavor, and conflict was part of the "small self" as compared to the "large self" that is the vastness of our potential. In her view, life was limitless. Once again I felt I was the student who wanted to know about the properties of the sun in all its magnificence, and instead I was being told to simply "enjoy the warmth."

Looking back, it is easy to see that I was shifting my point of view from outside myself, as though others knew better or more than I did, to a point of view that recognized the vast inner knowing that every human being is composed of within. The East on the medicine wheel was calling me to go within rather than to give away my knowledge and awareness to someone else. However, the battle in my mind was evidenced by the two words, "domination" and "dominion," and the two combatants were the Nagual and Carlos Castaneda.

Carlos Castaneda described the world through the eyes of a warrior, interested in the machinations of war, attentive to the "enemies" encountered on the path, battling sources that sought to defeat us. From this Nagual's perspective, Castaneda's tenets on the Toltec path were suspect because they involved a worldview of domination.

Despite the discussion between the two not being welcome, the Nagual made comments that clearly declared her stance: "Castaneda's route to freedom occurs by becoming a warrior. A warrior promotes domination, and that is not my choice for how to practice this path."

Yet in my years of studying Castaneda's material, I did not sense that either he or Don Juan were at war with anyone, or taking advantage of anyone, as the Nagual implied was evident from domination. I remembered a feeling of vigilance, the importance of being on one's toes. I remembered working to increase my awareness as much as I was able, lest I allowed the busyness, foibles, moodiness, and mundane qualities of daily life to suck me down and dry. It was the petty concerns of daily living that squelched spirit, it seemed to me. That was the arena where the battle took place, if there was such a thing.

Much of Toltec literature is written with "warrior" language: Tomas, in his concordance of Castaneda's work, lists over 300 terms beginning with the word warrior.[7] But before I got started listing the Nagual authors who used the word warrior, I saw that in the end I would only be attempting to fortify my position rather than presenting a sound argument for my point of view. Using words as weapons wasn't necessary or useful for either one of us.

Silent knowledge, knowing that arrives apart from the mind, settled the debate, in fact bypassed the debate altogether. Was an argument what I wanted? Yes and no. I needed to talk through varying perspectives because discussion allowed me to understand what was in my head. Yes, I know, the Nagual often said that "understanding is the booby prize," but I wanted the discussion not as a means to try to prove my point but as part of my process of learning. Debate would merely be a semantic way of discussing the differences.

Silent knowledge showed me that the two viewpoints – the way of the warrior as opposed to the way of love's dominion, are a duality. One is the opposite of the other, yet they are intimately connected. When you hold a coin between your fingers, you see the distance, if only in millimeters, between the two sides of the coin; however, you are not able to see the clear image on either side of the coin itself, even though the two sides are really not that distant from one another. Silent knowledge equalized the two sides of this particular "coin" – dominion and domination – by virtue of them being the same object with very little distance separating them. The same object, albeit viewed from two perspectives. If this were true, and silent knowledge indicated it was, there was something beyond both of them, something that held them both.

The ability to be fluid between both perspectives was being called for. In order to act from a position of non-duality, I needed to be flexible; whereas it had been too tempting to try to determine which position was the correct one and thereby I had also been missing the point altogether. Black or white wasn't a necessary position to declare, but the grays in between the two extremes was the best position to strive for.

Intent had brought me there to study with the Nagual. I was immersed in her point of view as intended by being there, just as I was still immersed in my previous view dominated by Carlos Castaneda. Whatever was beyond both of them was the position to strive for, yet what that was still was unknown to me. However, I would remain vigilant and aware, since grappling back and forth between the two was not proving to be helpful. In fact, it felt crippling.

I reminded myself inwardly to *be careful of demanding the need to define what is happening*. All of this had been rumbling and percolating for months. Encountering Cat and entering "silent knowledge" had allowed me the opportunity to see both sides of the coin. My task was to remain fluid between two seemingly disparate points of view.

May 10

Early morning was my time to do yoga. Afterwards, I would sit cross-legged on my bed with my back straight as a flagpole, focused softly at a point on the wall, and begin my meditation. I knew that the purpose of meditation was to clear the mind, but sometimes those thoughts and images scuttling just off the mind's screen as a meditation begins are worth paying attention to. That morning was one of those meditations, and the realization was a freighter full of knowledge: *The more I handle Power, the more I can read others' minds. Remember, Jess, Power is to be in a state of non-duality; it is the fuel needed for you to be in an optimal state of being.*

More and more often I was finding myself spontaneously knowing information about people. Boom! A basket of information would "drop at my door" from an anonymous "donor." The knowledge would show up out of the blue, at times as an outcome of focus, but the fact of knowledge suddenly coming to me had been happening with fair regularity. Without intending to know, a thought would pop into my head that was often about someone I was with. It also was happening when I was alone, which was the case on this particular morning.

It was different from my familiar way of viewing the world from a therapist's perspective; it didn't have that tag of hypothesizing, figuring out, even analyzing, as though I was working with a lost psychological puzzle piece that fit into a patient's story. It didn't have to have any relevance to the conversation at hand nor to any internal train of thought. Unexpectedly, I simply knew.

During that morning's meditation, the experience of mind reading was going to be linked with Power, and the pairing of those two disparate experiences was about to blow my mind. Then, because meditation slows mental processes, additional knowledge would be laid out in a clear and concise manner.

The image that comes in the meditation is of a harbor with loaded freighters edging up to the dock carefully and slowly. They've arrived at a foreign port that is crowded with fellow freighters, all vying for a boat-slip to unload their cargo. The freighters of awareness were about to fill the harbor of mind. The first freighter to pull up is the knowledge that Power enabled me to read minds.

The next freighter arrives and with it the awareness: *Once the knowledge comes to me, I feel responsible for the information.* The knowledge feels like a weight, as though the freighter is at full tonnage and I am responsible for what happens to the heavy load. I feel responsible to move the knowledge from one location to the next.

Silently, another freighter slips up to the dock: *How easy it is to take advantage of the ability to read others' minds and, in a sense, to manipulate.* My eyes widen as this freighter squeezes alongside the previous one. Ah! This is the seduction of Power. The dark side. "Power hungry" is when a good thing is turned bad by its inappropriate use.

Another freighter inches along into a space I hadn't imagined possible a moment before: *Impeccability is needed to handle Power.* I see that I need personal integrity and sobriety to deal with the knowledge that comes my way.

Impossible that there could be any room left for a final freighter, and yet it edges its way in despite the tight quarters: *Just because I know, doesn't mean I tell.*

After the meditation, I telephoned the Nagual, thinking, dryly, *Much easier than jumping into my car and driving down to Mexico,* as Castaneda felt compelled to do whenever he desperately needed guidance from Don Juan. The Nagual, I had discovered, was responsive to phone calls, more open to discussion over the phone than group discussions during the evening meetings. I was grateful for this.

"I call it eavesdropping," the Nagual explained after I'd shared my revelations. Relief flooded me. It was comforting to have the Nagual both understand what I was saying and provide me with an explanation for what was happening. "Reading people can either assist or become a deficit. It's an energy that needs to be handled in a neutral way rather than in a leading way. I have to be careful not to trap or to ask questions that I already have the answer to. To do that is not impeccable. I've learned, too, that reading people is easily influenced by my filters and biases, so I have to watch for that."

As the Nagual spoke, one last freighter shimmied into the dock of my awareness: *Nothing needs to be done with the knowledge gained from my massage relationship with the Nagual.* It remained in the dock of my mind. In other words, to have knowledge about the level of body knowledge she lacked wasn't anything I needed to share with her; that is, unless she was curious to know more about it. And at this point in our relationship she hadn't indicated to me that she wanted the knowledge I knew about her body.

May 27

Beyond Makiki, the town in which we lived, shy by maybe a mile, was lush green jungle. The network of trails through this tropical area was vast. It was well known by hikers, runners, and those who wanted to get away from the chaos of city life.

Early one morning, I talked Carla and Laurelle into walking one of my favorite trails. I had spoken to them of how the trail, the trees, the rocks, and the animals spoke to me, but apart from that I wanted them to see the beauty that surrounded us so close at hand. Carla had flown in from New York a week earlier. We'd been enjoying time together as a family, and she was scheduled to leave in the next day or so.

The well-marked trail began behind a ranger station at the end of a steep valley and the ascent started immediately. There were dozens of such valleys on the island, all vertical folds of igneous rock coated with red earth and seeded with greenery. Many of the plants and creatures there are endemic to the island, and as many had arrived by stealth, cargo, or air years ago. It was rare that the ground underneath the foliage was dry, therefore, the trail was moist, smelling of wild orchids, lilikoi, guava, and oftentimes, decay and musty humus.

Fifteen minutes up the trail we reached a grove of thin, spindly eucalyptus that dotted an internal spine of the valley. (Later, an aged hiker informed me that the eucalyptus had been planted at the end of WWII as a means of preventing soil erosion, without knowing at the time that the oil in the droppings from the tree prevented anything from growing underneath them.) Hundreds of the thin, closely planted trees dotted the ridge. Their exposed roots covered the area with gnarled, knobby tendrils of hardened wood that was barren and slippery. It was the barest part of the trail that boasted the quickest gain in altitude. For those hiking the trail for exercise, it was a heart-pounding stretch. Midway, I called out for the girls, who were hiking slightly ahead of me.

"Hey, girls! Stop a minute," I called. The trail had been speaking to me, and surprisingly, it was about them. My heart was racing. I had hiked the trail enough to know that my racing heart was not from the incline; it came from the conversation with the trees.

"The reason I want you to be with me is because I love to have you with me," I said. That sounds patent for a mother, doesn't it? The comment came from their earlier grumbling: "Mom, hiking is your thing, not ours, but we'll go because we know you want to share it with us. Just remember it's not going to be a regular thing. After all, how interested are you in lying on the beach?" Their point was a salient one.

Without countering their argument, I continued straight to the heart of what the trail had been saying to me.

"I've invested so much into raising you. I'm proud of you, and I like to show you off by being with you." (Ah, this is why Catholics have a barrier between themselves and the priest when they confess! Eye-to-eye can be intimidating.) "When you have kids you'll understand in a different way than you do now," I ended lamely, knowing that my last comment had been a defense of my position.

Carla and Laurelle watched me intently and said nothing.

"In fact, you two represent my total investment of time, effort, and attention for the past twenty years!" This realization had just broadsided me a few minutes before, while ladder-climbing up and over the knobs and twisted roots at my feet. It was the reason my heart was pounding, and I felt the beads of sweat planted on my forehead. The change in perception of who and what I perceived myself to be had been as sudden as the rise in altitude.

When the girls behaved in certain ways, I had a difficult time accepting their choices. Their choices indicated to me that my "investment" may have flaws, it may have weaknesses, pointing to the conclusion that I didn't do as complete a job in raising my daughters as I liked to think I did. I needed them to act in such a manner as to bolster my story that I'd made a good investment. To add injury to insult, that belief locked them into acting according to those same expectations. I had burdened them with my own expectations in the name of "love."

Remembering the Nagual's koan, "Carry the rock and not the weight of the rock," I realized that an experience could be unnecessarily weighted down by expectations and assumptions. But if the experience is free of those same expectations and assumptions, it's a very different experience. In fact, it can be so different as to provide a sense of weightlessness and freedom.

Yes, I loved my daughters! No, I didn't want my "love" to be a form of payoff for the effort I'd made in raising them. They needed to be free of me. I needed to be free of them. Only then were they truly free to make the decisions that young adults make. Only then could I make decisions free from the role of parent and mother.

All of this I said in a rush, the words spilling out of me like marbles tumbling out of a leather pouch. Never before had I seen the energetic fibers that bound me to my girls in the form of my investment in them. Never before had I seen what a crippling thing it was for them to be burdened with my "love." A gust of wind blew among the trees and I stopped talking. I looked away from the girls and let the wind soothe me.

"I wish I had my pipe with us to do a ceremony," I said, sighing. Carla spoke up.

"You love your ceremonies, Mom. We don't need a pipe. Look! The freedom is ours! Right now." I reached for the waist of each girl on either side of me, and we continued our hike up the valley of the talking trees.

May 31

"I'd like you to share your thoughts, feelings, and concerns about the Center," the Nagual addressed the Thursday night group. Over the previous six months the Nagual had mentioned this same topic on several occasions. As a group, we had made suggestions as to how we could boost the income at the Center in order for the Nagual to keep it open. She had warned us in the past that if she were not able to get additional income, her only option would be to close shop. Past suggestions for action were brought back to the table, with discussion on each. New suggestions were made. Hesitant to speak, I sought for an omen. Should I speak up or remain silent? Quicker than I ever imagined possible, the inner response came: *Speak up!*

"I'm going to take a risk," I ventured to the group. "What I'm about to say might not sound helpful in a practical way..." I paused and plunged forward like a diver who propels his body off the board too late to stop once the toes were lifted. I aimed my words at the Nagual, for it was there the impact was going to be felt, I suspected.

"Many of the comments made in the past several months have addressed ways to keep the Center open. These are helpful, and I know you've looked into some of them, but I don't think they address all of what may be going on." I paused again. Like fingers breaking the surface of the water upon impact, my words reached their target.

The Nagual's eyes were on me, not in a casual manner, but in a "don't mess with me" stare. Quickly, I plunged into the deepest depths of the pool while my confidence was still intact. Those eyes spoke volumes, but I was not backing down.

"The Center staying open is about you," I said, "about something going on within you, not about us finding ways to keep it open for you. Six months ago you told us that you set your

Intent to keep it open. Something needs to shift inside you for it to stay open." No one spoke. The Nagual's eyes bore into me. She used her eyes like a Samurai uses his sword. She sighed. Then she began to speak as I resurfaced from the depths my words had taken us to.

The Nagual spoke of the months and months it took to clean the Center from the squalor she had found it in, to paint the entire building inside and out, to install new carpet, to decorate each room with items that fit their purpose. She'd done all of the work we could see by glancing around us. She spoke of her dream for it to become a Center for healers of all persuasions, a sanctuary where they could practice their art. She spoke of the first group of students that had come and how they had left under factions of unrest. She spoke of never fully gaining an understanding of why things had ended so badly. She spoke of the death of her dream looming over her in the past six months. She wasn't able to pay the rent for much longer, supported solely by her current endeavors.

I was transfixed by the Nagual's admission. Her passion filled the room as she spoke. She wasn't lecturing; she was sharing an experience that had moved her beyond the concerns of daily living that easily robbed us of our vision. No one moved, no one interrupted. Our ears were attuned to every word. Not often did the Nagual share her vulnerabilities. Her love for this dream was palpable, all that she'd nurtured and cared for and grown with every investment she knew to give. Her sadness and longing that the dream had yet to be fully realized was mixed with love. Her near defeat prompted her one more time to ask her students and apprentices for help. The Nagual stopped, the mother who had dreams for her infant and cradled the vision close in her heart. She indicated to take a break before gathering together for the evening meditation.

That's when I made a second high dive with the intention of approaching the Nagual and sharing with her the synchronicity

I was seeing between my hike days ago and the discussion that night. The two had a powerful direct link. To share what the trail had said to me felt paramount. The expectations I had for my daughters were keeping them bound to me. I was carrying the weight of my expectations as a mother into my relationship with my adult daughters, and then shortchanging them by holding them to those unspoken agreements. Not only did they need their freedom, but I needed mine, too.

The parallels to the Nagual's feelings about the Center felt like a mirror reflection to feelings about my family. She was attached to her expectations for the Center. She was placing the responsibility for the solvency of the place on the shoulders of her students and apprentices. The congruence of those two attachments in our lives was a perfect example of the Nagual's koan, "There is no out there." Her inadequacy in her own ability to finance the Center compelled her to ask her students for the wherewithal to keep it open just as my inadequacy in accepting my daughters' behaviors kept me attached to them in an unhealthy manner.

As I spoke these parallel processes aloud to the Nagual, I longed for her and I to support each other in our similar endeavors. I longed to feel connected to her by our interest and passion for freedom apart from our joint dependencies. *We can be allies together!* I thought. *We can assist and support each other on this path that isn't always as clear as we'd like it to be. We are the active agents in both of our situations, the people with the ability to respond – not grown children, not students and apprentices. Our joint passion for what we devote ourselves to in our lives can be a connecting link to the journey we are on and to each other. The bridge we could forge together on our quest for freedom was here in our similar experiences.* These were my thoughts that I was unable to articulate quickly enough before I saw the Nagual's reaction.

The look on her face wasn't difficult to read. She was vacant. Her smile was plastic. Not one more word was spoken. Her vulnerability, love, and passion had been stuffed away into a container labeled "Private." I excused myself to end the encounter. I had overstepped my role in our relationship. I had traversed boundaries which, though unspoken, were clearly drawn by the vapid look in her eyes and by her thin, pursed lips.

Defeated, a balloon with no air, I lay down on the carpet and waited for the meditation to begin. Our relationship wasn't going to have the reciprocity I longed for. Sadness permeated my walk home in the darkness of the early summer evening.

June 13

Marianne and I agreed to meet in town for a cup of coffee at a small, outdoor café. As the new program director for Program IV, she asked that we meet weekly, since I was the clinical therapist for the program. This was our first meeting. The agency had recently opened up several residential programs for a difficult mental health population: children with behavioral challenges who were in the state's care and who no longer fit into the educational system due to their unique needs. Three homes had been established: one for elementary school boys, one for elementary school girls and one home for a single young girl with severe behavioral challenges.

My role as therapist was to meet with the kids in the program individually each week in order to "do therapy." A broad definition of doing therapy with emotionally "challenged" youths was that the therapist was to guide and direct them to make better choices, and to mentor them in what those choices ought to be. The role was one of educator, mentor, and expert. The kids were required to meet with me if their behavior was deemed severe enough. Turned out I was meeting with most of the kids in the program.

My approach to doing my job didn't align with the common mode of treatment for this population. In my view, these kids had been "over-serviced." They'd had plenty of specialists in their lives telling them what, why, when, where, and how they needed to conduct their lives. I met with each kid on a regular basis, mindful that they didn't need another adult telling them what to do. Listening closely to what their needs were at that moment in time, I sought to meet their immediate needs, whether to coach, interpret, redirect, support, or simply listen. That was the expertise I brought to the relationship.

I might do one or all of those things, but foremost I accepted that the kid I was with was directed to me by *Intent*. Intent is the creative force that we tap into to guide our lives. It is the clarity that comes with direct knowledge from the Universe, having little to do with information gathering or decision-making or research data. It didn't matter whether or not the kids were aware of Intent or whether or not they wanted to *do* therapy, I met them in the moment. Given that premise, our moments together were vital to their well-being and to my own as well. We had a job to do together, and it was a joint effort, in no way directed by my "expertise" alone. They contributed equally to the moment at hand. I communicated this to them. I wanted them to be aware of the possibilities and the potential for the time we spent together each week. What happened during our time together was ours to create.

What became apparent as I was talking with Marianne was that I had never really shared with her my feelings, thoughts, and opinions about the position of therapist because there hadn't yet been the opportunity. The way I did therapy with the kids in the program didn't track with evidence-based treatment modalities common for work with school-aged kids. I was eager to share with her why I thought the modality I used was effective. She listened and asked questions to clarify and to elaborate further on why I used the approach I did.

I used Daphne as an example. Daphne was a young girl who had experienced sexual abuse by relatives for years before she was removed from her home and placed in a residential home. I was the therapist in that home. Daphne struggled with her sexual identity at nine years of age. She wanted to identify herself as bisexual but experienced a great deal of ambivalence and angst due to her feelings for her female peers. She was aware of her previous sexual abuse, but like many nine-year-old girls, her interests were in peer relationships. Her stay in the residential facility was tenuous due to the difficulty she experienced with her behavior and social interactions. She had difficulty with following a daily schedule, with self-care, with staff interactions, with schoolwork, and with social skills.

All the while this extreme behavior was evident in the home, Daphne would talk to me of how she couldn't seem to make Trinity (another young girl placed in the facility) like her or play with her or share her toys. This inability to make friends caused Daphne much grief and anxiety. She could not care less about whether or not her bed was made in the mornings or whether or not she got her spelling words correct, but she was distraught when Trinity shunned her. My approach as the home therapist was to talk with Daphne about how she was feeling each day that I met with her, to find out what the most salient point of connection could be between us, and to assist her in problem solving for that day. Reminding her of the house rules, pointing out how she'd failed to meet staff directives, or running through a list of appropriate behaviors expected from her was futile, even though these things were what the staff wanted me to do.

The point of contact for any conceivable change was the moment at hand for Daphne. The most power for change was the moment when she felt connected, and so most likely to hear anything I might have to say. That moment was my guide for how to interact with her. My responsibilities as the therapist were to be fully present when I met with Daphne, to discover with her what her needs were for the day, and to find a way for her to be successful despite her challenging upbringing. I brought my expertise to the table each time I met with Daphne and I expected for her to bring her "expertise" as a kid to me; in other words, to meet with me weekly and engage in the moment at hand.

Paralleling my thoughts about my job were my thoughts, feelings, reactions, and opinions as an apprentice to the Nagual. My role as an apprentice was to avail myself of all the Nagual had to offer. This included both of her weekly evening meetings, the monthly activities that took place at different locations on the island, the monthly Sunday gatherings at the Center, and her guidance and teachings in general. I was seated as her apprentice because Intent had opened the way for me to be there. My contribution to our time together as an apprentice was as important as her contribution in the role of Nagual.

If I were to be responsible – physically, emotionally, and energetically – if I remained open-minded, committed to our joint experience, and followed her suggestions as much as I was able, then I would be maximizing my time with her as an apprentice.

I didn't want to miss anything, but something was amiss. I felt I was doing my part as an apprentice but I was uncertain about how the Nagual engaged with me and with others. Yes, she provided a lecture on Tuesday and Thursday evenings. Yes, she provided activities once or twice a month. But what was missing?

I observed the topics of conversation the Nagual had with her other apprentices. Their engagement was most lively when discussing areas of relationship difficulties in their lives rather than discussion of Toltec techniques or how using those same techniques could impact daily experiences in their lives. Focusing on relationship issues allowed the Nagual to instruct, guide, inform, lead, and counsel. This was the format for conversation she appeared to be most comfortable with.

However, therein was my beef: the group had the feel of a therapy group. I didn't want to sit around with these women as some of them used the Nagual as their therapist. I came to the Nagual to gain knowledge and experience on the Toltec path. But I found myself with a Toltec Nagual who was comfortable running a group that looked suspiciously like a therapy group. I wanted something different. Not right. Not wrong. Just different. And yet…

Marianne was not requesting that I change how I was working with the young kids in the program and use evidence-based treatment modalities instead. She wasn't pointing out to me that significant research had been done on the most effective means of successful treatment, nor the fact that I wasn't using those modalities. She wasn't demanding that I work with the kids in any specific manner. She accepted my work. Could I accept how the Nagual was "nagualing"?

June 22

Steady rain pattered on the driveway alongside the house next to my bedroom windows. I had been sound asleep but suddenly woke up. Nothing that I could determine had awakened me, but my body was wakeful and tense, the tenseness that signaled a state of perception. Mind asleep and body awake – the same perceptive state I'd been in during visits with the Cat.

Suddenly, a woman appears at the foot of my bed. She flows from the right side of the bedroom to the left toward the bedroom door, as though she were a ghost. I wonder how she came to move in that direction, since there are no door on the right side of the room. Had she been standing at the windows listening to the tapping rain while I slept? I don't feel threatened; instead, I feel a sense of reassurance and comfort.

Whoa. I figure it is the same woman who had lain down next to me just a few days previously. In fact, it has been less than a week since I'd wakened in the same manner to feel a woman nuzzle against my back as I lay in bed. I had automatically assumed it was Laurelle, that she must not be feeling well and so had climbed into bed with me. Her body had been warm, almost feverish.

I concentrate on speaking to the woman who has appeared at the foot of the bed, but my voice won't utter a sound. The vocal cords feel paralyzed. With great difficulty, I force the words out of my mouth, "Are you okay?" The sound is guttural, grainy; nothing more comes out.

No response. The woman is the same woman though! I can't determine how I know, and I can't speak coherently. The woman's shape is nondistinct. Rather than being feminine in shape, her body is an upright, oblong with a rounded top, like someone who has a sheet over their head. Her color is honey gold, a color that warms me deep inside, like one feels within minutes of drinking a latte. Toasty warm. I wake to realize I had been dreaming.

Laurelle got home a little later at 2:30am. I heard the car being driven with caution down the long driveway next to my bedroom windows. The headlights pierced through the darkness. She slipped into the bedroom door whispering, "Mom?"

"What's up, sweetie?" I asked. Laurelle didn't normally wake me when she came in at night.

"I got stopped by a policeman on the way home," her voice had alarm in it. I waited. She didn't normally put herself into compromising situations with regards to drinking, but neither had she awakened me to report she'd gone dancing at a club. Her story wasn't yet told.

"I was so nervous. I'd had two drinks early in the evening. They'd set cones along the street right outside the club, and they were stopping all kinds of people as they pulled out of the parking lot. Shitty they do that coming out of a club, don't you think?"

I couldn't really answer for the rationale in a policeman's mind. "Did you find the registration and insurance in the car?" I asked. "They're in there."

"Yeah, I found it, finally. Glad I was driving your car, not mine, since I don't have insurance yet on mine." Laurelle's voice had lost the edge of fear.

"By the time I found the registration and insurance, the policeman said, 'I suggest you keep your paperwork together next time, young lady,' and he waved me on. He didn't even do the sobriety check." She sounded both annoyed with the policeman and relieved.

"I'm glad he didn't do it. Glad as well that you were in my car. Let's call and get your insurance tomorrow, okay? You've had the car a month now, and it's time to stop putting it off."

So that was her scare. I lay in bed wide awake in a state of heightened awareness, a state of super-duper clarity. Seemed to me that Laurelle had set up the entire scene for herself, including successfully meeting the driving expectations for a young adult just leaving a nightclub. Furthermore, for whatever reason, she appeared to need to spot-check herself. Given there is "no out there," she'd used a policeman to keep tabs on her behavior. Seemed it made her feel responsible and trustworthy.

And then as a further extension of those realizations, I did a Byron Katie on myself: *What experience have I had in the past few days in which I needed a "spot check"?* Easy answer: Lots of negative, judgmental, critical thoughts and feelings had been running me ragged. All the way from, "I can't relate to anything the Nagual is saying," to, "What in the hell am I doing as a forty-something-year-old woman following this path?" I didn't often go to those depths anymore. Initially, that type of thought had raked me over the coals but not in a very long time. A fissure had opened up, allowing all kinds of critical thinking to erupt.

The previous week, while driving on the H1 Freeway into Honolulu, a small bumper sticker on a car adjacent to me had caught my attention. Actually, it had hit my visual cortex in neon: "Think Differently," it had read.

The next morning, I awakened early to go hiking. The overnight rain had soaked the trail but that didn't stop me from going. Draping a light raincoat over my shoulders, I began the trail. Neither had the rain dampened the spirits of other die-hard hikers. The trail was crowded as usual. One woman hiked fifteen paces behind me the entire time.

An impetus to keep moving, she hiked along at a steady pace with her umbrella covering her shoulders. The trail was slippery as I pushed myself up and over the familiar roots and rocks on the ridge. I listened behind me to the slosh, slosh of my fellow hiker. Think differently.

I thought about the wonder of a daughter who exhibits more than a decent measure of maturity for her age. I thought about the wonder of a woman, without form, visiting me in the night, warming up my entire being. I thought about the mystery of Intent bringing me to Hawaii to study with a Nagual who was so very different from me.

June 25

The topic for the evening lecture was two terms common to the Toltec student: "dreamers" and "trackers." It was a topic I was eager to hear the Nagual speak about because these terms were fundamental to following the shamanic path. The Nagual began her lecture.

"The traditional Toltec tools used by shamans to help navigate the world are 'dreaming' and 'tracking.' Tracking is interchangeable with the term 'stalking,' but I prefer the term tracking because it has less of a predatory tone. The practice of these two skills is a means of gaining information and building personal power. They're used for divination but they're also used as a practical means for daily living. There are pros and cons to both skills.

"Tracking is the art of observing yourself and your world, including people, places, and things, and then making decisions based on what is observed. The skill of tracking is often used in relationship to others. It's the skill of knowing how to best interact with what is happening around us. The tracker is an observer of human nature and oftentimes the tracker's intuitive observations are uncannily accurate. For the tracker, it isn't uncommon to have knowledge about a situation but to be unaware of how they came to have that knowledge.

"The dreamer is no less astute but comes to their knowledge while dreaming. The dreamer sees the world in pictures and images; however, they can run into difficulty when they interpret their dreams through their own filter systems. The dreamer needs to develop lucid dreaming as a means of harnessing Power."

My hand popped up. "How do I develop my dreaming capacity?" I had practiced tracking skills since beginning to travel the Toltec path, and tracking fit in handily in my work as a therapist, but lately I had suspected that I was really a dreamer. Maybe the Nagual could help me distinguish between the two.

"By paying attention to your dreams," the Nagual responded. Undaunted by her brief response and realizing that my question may have been as ambiguous as her reply, I continued.

"I don't have any trouble dreaming. I dream often and I've worked with my dreams for years. What I have trouble doing is consciously going into lucid dreaming; it happens randomly rather than on purpose."

"To lucid dream you need to set your Intent. Also, problem solve your question by asking a dream to give you the answer."

"Ah! I never thought of asking my dreaming skill for help in order to dream better," I mused aloud.

"Use your stronger skill of tracking inside the dream," the Nagual continued.

Hmm, I thought to myself, *I would do that if I could be more aware in my dreaming. What keeps me so busy in my dreams that I have so little energy to stay aware?* I wondered. Suddenly, I grasped the answer and spoke aloud as though everyone had been following my train of thought.

"What happens in my dreaming is that I fall in love with the story and get stuck there. I may be lucid, but I become absorbed with the dream and don't move on from it." I'd never connected the two before: the story of the dream dominated my attention so that I stayed put in the dreaming details. Essentially, I got trapped in the story of the dream.

"That's a pitfall of dreaming," confirmed the Nagual.

That evening I set my Intent: to ask the dream state how to dream differently, how to develop my dreaming beyond my current dreaming practices.

Early the next morning, I had a vivid, intense dream. It wasn't a dream I had to run after to remember, or a dream that was full of detail and went on for a long time with lots of twists and turns. Nor was it a dream with decorum. It was a dream that may bring a blush to tell, but it was a dream full of Power, saturated in the cohesion of the physical body with the dreaming body, giving me not a story to get stuck in but a complete surrender to dreaming potential.

In the dream, I am waiting for a program to begin. The program holds little significance beyond my attendance, and so I am sitting, waiting, and bored. I begin to pleasure myself and am soon fully aroused. Being in such a state of sexual awareness is one of the most intoxicating, alive, and complete states one can be in. It requires complete surrender, and it is one of the most effective means of moving the assemblage point.

There are other means of moving the assemblage point as well: meditating, hallucinogens, distance running, exhaustion, and extreme hunger. But my dream didn't involve me in any of those. It involved me in sexual climax. I was both awake and asleep at the same time and in a state of non-duality. Instantly, I knew that my intent to develop my dreaming capacity to its fullest extent had been answered. The answer was in the state of non-duality that was present for the surrender to take place in the first place. No filters. No expectations. No storyline to trap my attention.

Throughout the day at work, troubling images began to pop up in my awareness: images of prostitution, exploitation, human trafficking, misuse of the sexual relationship, sexual perversion, and so on. All of these activities are rampant social misuse of the inherent Power of sexual energy. In contrast, in its unadulterated state of surrender, sexual energy can take us to our core where we find the storehouse of our body's energy source.

Wasn't this the very experience I'd had with Cat? When I'd surrendered to Cat and offered it worship in effect I'd acknowledged the Power at the core of who I am. This latest experience had been a bit different, in that it had been enveloped in sexual nuance, but at its core the experience was the same. Surrendering to the Power of who I am was an act of non-duality and was at the heart of why I'd come to Hawaii in the first place.

In addition, I saw that this state of surrender led to developed dreaming. I knew it as a tracker and I knew it as a dreamer. There was no story, only surrender. The state of surrender was also the place in the East on the medicine wheel that brought with it new life and new knowledge. The Nagual had told me to surrender to the group, but what I was learning instead was my need to surrender to myself and trust in the knowledge that the surrender would bring.

July 6

On the tip of the island of Oahu where west meets north, the road ends. A mile or two before the end of the road is strictly four-wheel-drive access. Plenty of people attempt to drive it without four-wheel drive, thinking that their vehicles can manage the potbellied road. Nonetheless, it was surprising how many vehicles were on it this day, unable to go further due to the extreme holes that randomly pocketed the hard-packed road.

Leaving several cars at the end of the asphalt road, all thirteen of us had piled into the bed of Liz's huge Ford truck. It was our once-a-month outing, and we were going to spend the day hiking around the pencil point of the island to a cave on the opposite side. Most of the people in the truck knew each other. We were the regulars at the Center. However, at monthly outings others joined us who came irregularly, and they always added a fresh perspective to any activity, like using tertiary colors on a paint palette.

Our vehicle was without four-wheel-drive, so at the very best we were going to drive as far as possible to lessen the distance of the hike to our final destination. Lucky for us the road was dry. If it had been raining, those holes would've been veritable sinkholes. In the end, even the dry holes won out and the truck bottomed out with the weight of its load.

"Everyone get out!" Liz exploded in exasperation, as she scrapped the underside of the truck for the tenth time. Those inside the cab informed those of us in the bed of the truck that her frustration had festered from the outset. Neither she nor her truck wanted to be there. Listening to the comments, apparently I wasn't the only one who wondered why Liz came to events when it appeared she didn't want to be there.

"My truck's not gonna make it with this weight," she had grumbled early on. But she had been urged on and cajoled for the use of her vehicle by the Nagual; and in any case, she hadn't refused until the tires began to spit out dirt and pebbles. Full pedal wasn't going to budge that truck. At the smell of burning rubber and the sound of her high-pitched, bawling demands, we scrambled out pronto.

"Who organized this?" Carol asked wryly, knowing full well who organized the once-a-month events. Comments followed quickly like angry hornets dive-bombing a threat to their nest. "She knew her truck wouldn't make it on this road; how come she agreed to drive?" "Hey, this energy doesn't feel good, things are too tense." The Nagual finally intervened and said we were having "engineering difficulties."

I walked away from the group. Months previous, on the weekend trip to a neighbor island, the same bickering had erupted from the same parties. This felt like a rerun. The Nagual soon reorganized everyone. Six or eight pushed the truck out of the rut, and the driver pulled it off to the side of the road. A decision was made that Liz would stay with the truck while the rest of us continued the hike on foot.

The dirt road ran parallel to the ocean. The waves hit the jagged strip of lava shelf that made up the beachfront with pockets here and there of sandy shore. It wasn't a shoreline suitable for surfing, but line fishing was popular, and people were camped out with fishing poles stuck in the lava bedding. Further back from the lava shelves were tide pools with golden sand and patches of dirt supporting rugged beach naupaka flowers and succulent ilima, favorite seaweed of the locals, that thrived in the arid landscape on this westernmost coast. The air smelled of sea, and the waves sprayed the lava shore, leaving tiny pockets of water that eventually dried to grainy sea salt with the change of tides.

We walked along the dirt road until the Nagual pointed to a lava rock wall built into one side of a small ravine running perpendicular to the waves. The wall was twenty feet tall and ran a length of maybe thirty feet; it led nowhere that we could determine. Facing the wall was a path that fish-hooked around both ends of the wall; and by following the ascending path, we ended up standing on top of the wall itself. The wall was an odd structure to be standing on oceanfront property. The only conclusion the group could come to regarding its purpose was as an ancient Hawaiian heiau. The heiau was a sacred site to the Hawaiian people and was often composed of a wheel made with lava stone, an altar, or a random gathering of stones such as the wall. Amongst the group, no one knew more about it than that.

"Look around you," instructed the Nagual. "I want you to pick up a stone that speaks to you." Waiting as everyone searched for a stone, she retraced her steps back down the ravine and stood at the base of the wall. Scaling down the side of the ravine after having chosen my stone, I was soon standing in front of the wall with everyone else.

"Become aware of what you do, over and over, just as the action of placing each and every stone of the construction in front of you was repeated over and over. Eventually those individual stones of your actions end up in a wall of this size. Feel the energy of this spot, the immensity of the wall as we stand in front of it. Be aware of what you carry with you that leads you to the same spot again and again. This self-created wall exists between you and the freedom that you long for, yet you are unable to get over or around it effectively.

"Now let's follow the path back up this way," the Nagual said, turning to lead the way around the wall once more. She clambered up the other side of the ravine, and within minutes was overlooking us as we scrambled up behind her. The perspective from the top made the wall look less challenging, easier to overcome.

"Now throw your stone off the wall," commanded the Nagual. "Realize that repeating the pattern over and over always ends in the same results. Do something different. Let the pattern go."

This was the Nagual's teaching at its best in a natural setting: she used what she came upon in nature as the object of her lesson. She spoke less on an outing than she did during class on Tuesday and Thursday evenings, when her routine was to lecture for forty-five minutes and then conduct a meditation with the singing bowl. I enjoyed the "object lessons" during our outings, even though there wasn't always clear direction between the purpose for the experience and the experience itself. The Nagual relied on the experience to speak for itself, it seemed to me.

Continuing our walk, we followed an adjacent road away from the beach and along the apex of the island, a path that hugged the edge of the rock monolith that formed the landmass of the island's west end. Walking for nearly two hours, we eventually arrived at a cave located immediately around the corner of the western tip of the island.

If you didn't know the cave was there, you could easily miss it. We took an indistinguishable path up a steep incline twenty-to-thirty feet away from the trail we'd been on, and then scrambled back down at a right angle to the path after the Nagual spotted the mass of stones that signaled the cave opening.

Entering the cave from alongside the cliff, we crawled down large rocks that tumbled fifteen feet down into the bowels of the cave. Once inside, we could hear the constant crashing of the waves muffled by the density of the earthen walls. The cave floor was composed of hard-packed dirt with scattered rocks and boulders sprinkled about. Clothing clung to the rocks here and there, weathered by the dank and salty air. Broken bottles were scattered throughout. The smell of urine permeated the edges of the cave where shadows dwelt alone.

Everyone fit onto the floor of the cave as we seated ourselves around a gathering of rocks, twigs, and palm fronds that looked roughly like a fire ring. Larger rocks were in the center of the ring and were tinged with black soot from fires long ago. Where the palm fronds had come from, I had no idea; there wasn't a palm tree in sight for miles.

The Nagual asked Malia to sing, her voice a strong nasally vibrato like water flowing over lava stones in a jungle stream, her tone perfect for Hawaiian chant. Malia didn't come regularly to the Tuesday and Thursday evenings; but when she did come, the Nagual asked for the honor of her song as a celebration of the event.

Part Hawaiian, Malia was a beautiful woman. She had thick, spongy, long dark hair that was often swept into a pile on top of her head. Her makeup was done with care and her smile came easy. Hawaiian heirloom bracelets clinked against each other along both arms. Her clothing fit well, as though once donned it merged with who she was. I wished she attended the Center more often.

Her voice rose and filled the cave with ancient Hawaiian verse. As she chanted, the energy of the cave filled me, sweet and deep and venerable, feeling feminine and nurturing at the same time. Filled with the cave's energy, I leaned toward the Nagual and whispered, "I'd love to spend the night in this cave! Can you imagine what we might learn here?" I was also filled with lore of shamans using caves as springboards into other worlds. Malia's chant, along with the energy of the cave, had transported me to the edge of those worlds, and I longed to stay overnight to enter them fully.

"Well, we'd have to bring a dog with us if we did," she considered. I remained quiet. A moment ago I had been seated with shamans around a warm fire in a damp cave, and the next moment the Nagual's practical comment burst my dreaming bubble. A dog might well protect us, but from what? What about Power? This was exactly the type of thing I longed to know. I wasn't suggesting that we be foolhardy, but wouldn't Power provide a way? If Intent initiated the act, it would lead us to "right" action, wouldn't it?

I said no more. But I set my Intent to return to the cave later to find out what it might teach me.

On the return hike, we took the lower road. The Nagual sensed that a tide pool was calling to her off the path that was clearly laid out with stones. Signs were posted for hikers to remain on the path in order to protect the nesting albatross and shore animals endemic to this westerly, windblown beach. One of the apprentices challenged her, "Hey, we're not supposed to go off the path. See that sign over there."

"It doesn't serve us," the Nagual's response was clipped. She headed off into the beach sand, and everyone, even the naysayer, followed.

Soon we arrived at a large tide pool. The size of a man-made pool, it lay amidst a black lava formation big enough that the opposite side effectively cut off the waves from breaking into it with wild, wind-torn abandon. The wind was crazy – a nonstop affair that pummeled the shore until only the most hardy of plants and animals could sustain a life in this landscape. The pool looked deep and had sea-green algae clumped in spots over its surface. Small rivulets of fresh seawater fed the pool at several breaks in the lava.

I couldn't help but wonder at the continuing agitation in the group. It was a therapist's bane at times to notice every shift in emotions, but I knew my own sense of agitation that accompanied meetings with the Nagual was consistent. I had long begun to wonder if being with the Nagual didn't evoke a significant shift in energy level, and a familiar way of interpreting that energy was "agitation." I felt it in me; I saw it in others. I also wondered about the depth of the Nagual's ability or willingness to share with her apprentices more about her daily life rather than her apprenticeship experiences from years previous. When conflict is felt in a group and not talked about, everyone feels it regardless of it not being brought out in the open. The tension becomes a big elephant in the room. It's easy to hone in on others' communication and relationship issues in lieu of sharing those same things about yourself. Trust me on this one; a therapist does it too easily. The Nagual didn't talk much about herself or her relationship with Liz, but everyone could feel the tension between the two quite easily. Case in point was the tension earlier between the Nagual and Liz over the use of Liz's truck.

Back to the tide pools...

The Nagual instructed each one of us to kneel in front of her as we stood calf-deep in the water. "Are you going to baptize me?" I teased, as she turned me around and instructed for me to lay prone. She then pushed me gently into the center of the tide pool. Instantly, I was enthralled. My body was weightless, my eyes were closed, and I couldn't hear a thing, not even the waves crashing close by. I was a chrysalis – enveloped in a cocoon of peace and tranquility. I lay still for a long time, aware that my body was gently moving with the ebb and flow of the tide inside the pool.

Suddenly, hundreds of tiny suckers attached themselves to my back. Flailing my arms like a windmill, I rose out of the water. "What's biting me?" I called out to no one, hearing the hint of fear in my voice. The Nagual smiled. "Oh, the Loch Ness Monster," she replied pithily. When I looked closely into the water, I saw schools of tiny, translucent fish swimming along. I wondered at how they had perceived me floating along in their watery world. At the very least, they had acted as though I could be a morsel to eat, large as I was in comparison to their small size.

The return walk to the truck was quiet. I walked behind the Nagual, following in her footsteps as I had at the volcano, slipping into her energetic tail stream. The truck was where we'd left it, with Liz fast asleep in the cab. We gathered around its empty bed and ate our lunch, much appreciated after a long morning hike and the nibble-fest we'd had in the tide pools.

For the return trip home, I was paired with Linda and Julie in their van. They would drop me off at the Center where I'd left my car early that morning. They were sisters and newcomers to the group. I was curious about them, as they were the newest members to attend regularly since I'd first come the previous fall. I was curious about whether their acclimatizing to the group mirrored my own; and if not, how they were experiencing the whole deal.

Their presence in the group was like adding lemon zest to a dinner dish, while the dish had been missing something not quite definable without that added sprinkle. They were curious in their attention and applied that curiosity to their comments. They attended all events and were eager to report their most recent Toltec adventures. Linda was usually the speaker between the two of them. They prompted a feeling of zeal and a tenacity to learn, and I enjoyed them immensely.

Julie spoke up after closing the van door. "During the meditation last week, I shared some of my meditation with the group but not all of it. The part I didn't share involved you." I was riveted, all ears.

"This is the part I didn't share. You were standing on the edge of a large cliff looking over to me as I climbed up the cliff wall. As I looked up at you, you began throwing huge boulders down on top of me." Julie smiled and paused as she saw the smile on my face fade. I waited to hear more.

"At first I was horrified to see you throwing the boulders, but when I looked at your face, I saw that there was no malice in your eyes. I kept climbing and soon, as the boulders rained down on me, I realized that since I was a being of pure energy, the boulders couldn't harm me in any way. You smiled and the look in your eyes said, 'You've got it! You know!'"

I didn't know what the meditation meant because that was for Julie to discern, nonetheless I was honored that she shared it with me. Then Linda and Julie asked what had brought me to study with the Nagual.

Now it was my turn to tell a story. No one had asked me this question before. I wasn't sure how to respond.

"Intent brought me here to be an apprentice to the Nagual," I began, but that sounded so cliché. I tried again by sharing some of the factors that had contributed to my decision to pick up and move across the ocean to pursue study with a Nagual, but again my comments sounded scattered and inconclusive. I made a third attempt. What it came down to as I listened to myself speak, pure and simple, was Intent.

With conviction, I spoke assuredly, "When I first started reading Toltec writers, I couldn't understand their vocabulary. I had no idea what the terminology meant. A dictionary was no help. As I started practicing what was written in the books, I started experiencing those words and I was ready for more.

"I came to study with the Nagual because it was the next step on my path, because I needed a teacher, because an unseen force set up the affairs in my life for me to be here. All of those things brought me here." Finally my words were matching what my heart was feeling.

We continued to talk the remainder of the drive back to the Center. We spoke of our dreams and desires, of what it was like to be a student, about attending classes, observing the dynamics of what went on during class, and what it was like to engage with the Nagual. The conversation was the first of its kind since last fall when I'd started as an apprentice. My long silence had been lifted.

Linda and Julie spoke of things I'd observed but had said nothing about to anyone. My time up to that moment had felt like solitary confinement. I had begun to feel crazy, sitting alone too long with impressions and feelings that were unsettling. As we talked I felt relief flow through me, as though a pressure valve had been turned to the left. I hadn't been aware of the strength of the backlog until I released it. How good it felt to talk with these two ladies! The drive home was like a cold beer on a hot and sweaty summer day.

Once again, I found myself reflecting on the expectations that as an apprentice I had on the Nagual as a teacher. I looked forward to the once-a-month gatherings with the Nagual. They were an opportunity to glean from the Nagual and from fellow apprentices their knowledge and experiences in the context of nature. Even when I recognized that it was easy to want the "bells and whistles" or the mind-blowing, flashy, sensational events, I also recognized that those types of events happened briefly and then were gone. It was easy to want more of those events, like the coffee addict wants their third cup of coffee in the morning. Those events gave a temporary high, but there was also the eventual low that came along afterwards. In the expectation that all activities have an explosive climax, the misleading message was that they were critical for growth. Even the coffee addict eventually comes to recognize that caffeine provides little nutritional value to the body.

Likewise as an apprentice, if I looked for the Nagual to provide an adrenalin rush, I would continue to look to her to provide that same rush during every outing. Instead, it was my responsibility to be available physically, spiritually, and energetically during our outings. When I came prepared in this manner, I always found something to gain from the experience regardless of the "wow" factor to the event.

July 9

Living in Hawaii the first eight months of that first year was a tight squeeze financially. You, dear reader, have probably picked up on that. Because of my anorexic wallet, I hadn't purchased anything to add to the wardrobe I'd brought with me when I'd first arrived. Yep, not one item of clothing! For those who don't buy clothes on a regular basis, another example might be no longer buying a favorite beverage, or going on a sugar fast, or staving off any new music for a period of nearly a year. It was done out of necessity, not discipline. No fun, but doable, although it hadn't occurred to me to try it before.

Something happened in the midst of that clothing famine that I hadn't seen coming ahead of time. Freedom! I had freedom from investing energy into my wardrobe, into shopping, and into spending money that I didn't have. I didn't see those benefits while it was happening, only in hindsight. I experienced the total freedom of non-engagement, a sense of detachment from those values that I'd never before considered as valuable.

Paying attention to my clothing was something I did because I enjoyed it. Yet due to circumstances, I had set those values aside and walked away. I'd never really considered that those beliefs about my wardrobe which I'd been immersed in for most of my life needed to be changed. During those eight months I had stopped the energy exchange between what I put on my back and how I viewed what I put on my back.

During my morning meditation, a parallel circumstance to the freedom of not investing in a wardrobe hit me: I hadn't spoken with anyone else at the Center about my experience of being an apprentice to the Nagual before my recent conversation with Linda and Julie. I had foregone buying clothes for an unusual period of time, and I had also foregone speaking with anyone about the uneasiness in my relationship with the Nagual.

This was important to me because I wanted to pay attention to the teachings from the Nagual rather than to grumble about her. Months previous when White Fox suggested I practice silence, I worked at keeping silent, and I hadn't engaged in any gossip among the rest of the students and apprentices although there was plenty to be heard if I had chosen to join in on those conversations.

Internal silence was also a goal. It wouldn't be a congruent state to remain silent outwardly if I was going to be chattering on and on inside myself about these same issues. Keeping silent had been tough. I wanted to talk, talk, talk to release the tension. In the past I had clients come to me as a therapist and share with me their dissatisfactions. A pattern I had observed in many clients was the desire to share burdens but a lack of desire to move on to solutions to those burdens. I didn't want to do the same thing with the Nagual, although I felt isolated in my internal world. What a boon the discussion with Linda and Julie had been!

Suddenly, the freedom in not talking became as evident as the freedom of not being concerned with my wardrobe. Not talking allowed me to be detached. The detachment provided a very different view than being in the midst of it all, the literary equivalent of "losing sight of the forest for the trees." If I immersed myself in talking, explaining, and discussing preferences and opinions, I would lose sight of the bigger picture, which was that I was there to learn from the Nagual.

White Fox had taught me that asking too many questions was a defensive tactic; it kept me from attaining inner silence. Staying detached was showing me that lots of talking was also a defense.

"Detachment" is a word that deserves a moment of evaluation. The term can be viewed from opposite perspectives, and when viewed from different perspectives the emphasis can be a hundred and eighty-degrees different. One perspective views detachment as undesirable, because it promotes isolation and lack of involvement. How can we gain the benefits of a situation if we don't enter it fully and immerse ourselves in the experience? But detachment from the opposite point of view teaches something different.

Detachment is a concept found in the East on the medicine wheel. The East is the direction of insight and rebirth. By detaching from objects, opinions, people, and ideas, we can see clearer, make better decisions, and take action without the influence of those attachments. When we see clearer, our connection with Intent is stronger. The East is also the direction that emphasizes practicality; and for those eight months that I didn't have the financial wherewithal to buy clothing, I learned the freedom of non-attachment in daily practical matters.

July 17

"We're going to do the meditation differently tonight," the Nagual announced, sporting a mischievous grin. "We're going flying," she added with aplomb. She could have stood up and taken a bow for as pleased as she sounded. "We're flying to the Pyramid of Khufu at Giza." She gave no other directions. The Nagual did not often direct the meditation, so I looked forward to meditating with a locale in mind. In addition, we didn't often journey as a group during the meditation, and I was looking forward to what might happen. Her next statement, however, wiped the smile from our faces.

"And we'll be in the same seating positions as last time; I'll pair you." The group let out a collective groan.

Everyone was positioned in a circle with a large crystal placed in the center. One partner sat cross-legged while the other put their head face up in the lap of the one who was seated. Ouch! Stay in that position for forty minutes and muscles become strained in the back and the neck with the closeness of the partner pushing the boundaries of personal space. Both participants would be involved in the meditation.

The Nagual motioned for me to be the seated partner, and I was relieved since I'd been the one lying down during the last meditation. She then took a seat on the side of the circle with the singing bowl in her lap. The Nagual was applying heat just as she'd announced she was going to do weeks ago. The Nagual began circling the mallet around the edge of the singing bowl. I went into a meditative stance quickly. The singing bowl was a familiar trigger for the apprentices to go into a journey or trance state, just as familiar to me as lying on my bed at home listening to a binaural beat audiotape.

Traveling straight up into the universe, I paused to look around and locate the Nagual, expecting her to be in open space flying with me. We were headed for Egypt, right? But I was alone. Oops! I jetted quickly back to earth to join the group. I know it might sound odd, but journeying in this manner didn't require eyesight. On the level of energy, or chi, I knew just as surely as if my eyes were open what was happening around me, and, in this instance, no one was with me. I returned to earth quickly to join the group.

As I approached the earth, I could feel the tug and pull of the "rings of belief" as described by Robert Monroe in his book, *Far Journeys*.[8] I hadn't expected to run into them since I hadn't been practicing my journeying in the manner that Monroe shared in his book or at his retreat center, The Monroe Institute, in Faber, Virginia. Those experiences had been another chapter in my life four years previous, so I was surprised to encounter the rings of belief on this journey.

According to Monroe, energy layers surround the earth like layers of an onion, except that these "onion layers" serve as entrapments, and we get stuck in them without recognizing them as a trap. For example, Monroe believed the whole arena of religion was located in one of the rings, the rings of our beliefs. He described how human beings get hooked into the rings and spend their entire lives within a very small portion of the universe. I had identified with him in that regards: for years I had remained in the ring of religion!

It took concentration and effort to free myself because the rings can be fascinating places to be, but I released with a *pop!* like the lid on a pressurized jar being opened for the first time.

I share this portion of the journey to highlight one of the fascinating things that happen while doing shamanic journeying: we may not go anywhere while we're journeying, at least in a physical sense, but our energy travels and that energy is the essence of who we are. It is worth paying attention to everything we see, feel, and hear while on a shamanic journey, because what we encounter has an impact on our etheric or energy body.

I looked around to locate the Nagual and the other apprentices. Where were they in proximity to the rings of belief? It took me a few minutes of solo flying, but eventually I found them flying together in a group not too far from land. They hadn't flown far enough away from the earth to be in close proximity to the rings. Yep! I had been excited to journey together as a group but had overshot our destination by a few million miles!

I joined the others as we followed the Nagual in flight to the Great Pyramid of Khufu at Giza. I'd never been to Egypt, neither in daily reality nor in a journeying state, so I was surprised to see an enormous green eye at the apex of the pyramid. It reminded me of the image on a dollar bill, with an eye at the pyramid's tip-top. Emerald-green beams radiated in hundreds of directions from the eye itself. The Nagual invited each of us to speak. I paused. Finally, with graveness bordering on fear, awe bordering on worship, and feeling like Dorothy speaking to the Great Oz, I said, simply, "Thank you." I had had no previous contact with this Third Eye, as I termed it in my mind, but I was unduly impressed. It reminded me of esoteric practice in which the practitioner meditates on the Third Eye, the space on the brow between our two eyes, in order to attain a higher consciousness. I felt honored to be in the presence of this Third Eye. The Nagual then changed directions of the journey by flying up into space.

Heading straight into the sun, the Nagual didn't turn to see if anyone was following her. I lost the sense of others around me as all my efforts concentrated on keeping up. While hiking at Mauna Kea on the Big Island, the Nagual had a wicked pace. Apparently while flying on a meditative journey, she traveled just as fast. Aiming for the very center of the burning orb, I flew straight in after the Nagual. There was no time for hesitation, although I wasn't sure what would happen to my physical body. Again, this was a strange reaction to journeying: I'm on a meditative journey originating in my mind, and yet approaching the fiery sun caused me a moment's hesitation. Would I burn up?

What would happen to my body? The immediate feeling I experienced wasn't of heat, as I'd expected, but more like dry ice. Immediately, too, the coldness obliterated me with a speed greater than the sun's heat would've ever done.

As I flew into the sun, I was reminded of the fact that we are made of atoms. In our physicality, we think our bodies are solid, but quantum physics has known for years that the atom is both particle and wave and does not have the density we assume it has as we go about our daily lives. As I flew into the epicenter of our known world, I was returning to the source of life, at least physical life, and immediately became aware that my consciousness survived the flight! The feeling was one of exhilaration! The recognition that the death of the physical body has no impact on the continuation of my consciousness was a feeling that has never left me.

I turned around to watch as the other apprentices began to fly into the sun. I began to check in as to everyone else's whereabouts: Ah! I saw Linda. Check. Then I saw Julie. Check. There's Barb and Barbara. Check. Hey! Where's Carol? I became worried for her. At times she had admitted to having difficulty doing meditations. "It's not your job to take care of her," I heard a voice direct me, the voice of my higher consciousness. I quit looking for Carol and continued flying. Then I realized that I couldn't locate the Nagual, either. She'd disappeared after flying into the sun. *Okay, not your job to locate her either,* I told myself.

Suddenly, I became aware of a lime-green lizard sitting on my shoulder. With sudden awareness, a knowing that was beyond information, I realized that the lizard, with no self-consciousness, had a greater degree of freedom than I did. Human beings got trapped and entangled in the details of what happened in their daily lives, in the rings circling the earth, as Monroe had observed, more than the animals or plants did. "Consider the lilies of the field, how they grow; they toil not, neither do they spin."[9] The biblical admonition returned to me as though blessing the appearance of the lime-green lizard.

The sound of the singing bowl signaled the return to the Center. How I loved the sound coming from that bowl! It captured my attention like nothing else. Enraptured by the sound, I regretfully returned to self-awareness as the Nagual played the bowl to its highest pitch and then eased her circling hand to a slower speed. The sound mellowed. Everyone in the circle eased out of their positions and stretched. Groans rose from those lying down.

"My neck," someone moaned, and those who'd been seated responded with, "My back," until everyone was laughing at each other's discomfort.

"Hey, where'd you go in the middle of flying?" Carol asked the Nagual.

"Oh, I got up to put water in the fountain for a few minutes," she answered drolly. Several apprentices mentioned her disappearance in the midst of the group journeying, and we laughed at her indifference. Cheeky Nagual!

July 22

Dialing the Nagual's number as early in the morning as I dared, I held my breath. The phone rang, once, twice, and finally, "Hello" on the other end.

I sighed with relief and identified myself, then, bypassing any further telephone etiquette, I launched into the reason for my call. It'd been a sleepless night.

"I was reading *The Art of Dreaming*[10] after you'd mentioned it in class last night," I began. "I read it several years ago, and it didn't make any sense to me back then. I guess I wasn't yet advanced enough in my dreaming," I spoke rapidly, as though this was preliminary information. My sense of urgency was being driven by a number of realizations I'd had the previous night when it had been too late to call the Nagual. As mentioned earlier, I knew a goal for the apprentice on the Toltec path was to develop their dreaming capacity, because dreaming increased available Power in their lives. I also knew that using our nighttime dreaming in an active rather than a passive manner was another goal. By being active in "the Dreamtime" as Australian shamans called it, we would increase the flexibility and functionality of our etheric or energy bodies. All of this use of active dreaming lent the apprentice the opportunity for greater non-duality, hence freedom, in their lives.

"But in my reading last night," I went on, "I realized that according to Castaneda's definitions of the dreaming gates, I've passed the first two. If I follow his sequencing, then I should soon be visited by inorganic beings while dreaming."

I paused to catch my breath and felt the flush of blood traveling through narrow veins. "Inorganic beings" was a major component of Carlos Castaneda's Toltec cosmology. The Nagual had mentioned them for the first time in her recent lecture, although it wasn't clear whether or not she'd had contact with them. For Carlos Castaneda, an inorganic being was an energy that became present while dreaming, that had the potential to either completely deplete or completely energize the dreamer's energy body – they were *that* important. And my dreaming capacity was developing to the point that they would show up soon, if they hadn't already.

Next came the crux of my call: "Do you have the energy to watch over me?"

"Yes, I do," spoke the Nagual calmly, "but ultimately you make the decision as to how involved you want to be. It seems to me Castaneda got pulled into the inorganic beings' world. It's even probable he may have become one. Their allure is powerful. They've come to me many times and offered lots of things. I've always said, 'Thanks, but no thanks.'"

"I wonder if being drawn to Castaneda won't influence me to make some of his same decisions." Still breathless, I paused.

Fear weighed heavy on me, an albatross around my neck. My devotion to Castaneda had been complete before coming to Hawaii, and even though I'd pulled away from his ideology, I recognized the danger in dreaming. Here I was talking to the Nagual about someone she herself didn't align with, but I trusted her to get through that "onion layer" of belief and help me.

Fear was riding me hard. Whether we know it or not, whether we agree with it or not, our ideologies determine the quality and freedom in our lives. The "rings of belief" expounded by Robert Monroe weren't just something he discovered by being one of the first pioneers in the United States to go out of body and to proclaim the freedom in doing so. Shamans had done it for centuries, as did Carlos Castaneda. But the downside of dreaming in other realities begins with the doorway of fear, and fear can paralyze us to the point that we go nowhere at all.

"That's the risk you take in aligning yourself with him," the Nagual said plainly. "I think Castaneda allowed himself to get involved with energetic beings in other worlds, thinking he could pull out. In the end, I'm not sure he did."

Relief flooded me. I'd rushed to finish reading *The Art of Dreaming* in the last day, and my conclusion had been the same: Castaneda had succumbed to the power and allure of dreaming. I didn't know much about inorganic beings, but I was at a point in my own dreaming in which the temptation to access different worlds while in that dream state was present despite knowing it had proven to be Castaneda's downfall. The downright scary thing about the whole deal was that I wasn't convinced Castaneda knew about his own demise. He had been that caught up in his own dreaming prowess.

Relief continued to flow through me. "Well, at least I contacted you rather than him," I blurted out, a backhanded compliment if there ever was one. It may not have sounded all that comforting to the Nagual to learn that I was in an ongoing debate between her point of view and Castaneda's experiences, but my decision to ask her for support and guidance was an important one. By calling and speaking with her, I was placing my allegiance in her. I was surrendering to her directives.

"Just let me know what goes on in your dreaming, okay?" she replied.

As the call came to an end, I felt the fear continue to flow out of me as the tears rolled down my cheeks and dropped onto the bed sheets. I hadn't realized before speaking with the Nagual how seductive dreaming was yet how strongly I was attracted to it on a nightly basis.

July 25

I awake into a lucid state while dreaming and find myself in a bedroom full of vibrant color. The walls are painted turquoise, a collection of Mexican ceramic ware placed on rough-hewn shelves painted crimson, banana yellow, sapphire, and chartreuse. The window is opened wide, letting in a summer breeze. Curtains move in and out with the tempo of the breeze as though they are inhaling and exhaling, breathing life in and out of the room. An armoire is placed diagonally in the far corner facing the bed. I glance to either side of me and for the first time notice that several men are lying in bed with me.

Wide-awake, I know I am dreaming. So wide-awake, in fact, that details stand out in exquisite relief, color breathes with a life of its own, and the bedroom holds energy like no place I'd ever been. No exaggeration. This presence of palpable, visceral energy is always a clue that I am dreaming. The objects didn't matter; the people didn't matter – when that dreaming essence is present, the dreaming is always magical and powerful.

Another man approaches the side of the bed. Unlike the men lying next to me, he is clothed. Leaning forward, he reaches with a hand toward my legs. His gesture is neither aggressive nor sexual. So what did he want? As he leans toward me, I half wake. The room gets fuzzy and the intense color begins to fade. I am losing the cohesion of the dream state.

You were dreaming. Go back to that room, I urged myself. I lay perfectly still in order not to add one more risk factor that might prevent me from returning to the dream.

The room reappears in its original intensity. I glance around to see that now there are different people in the room. Ah! I am an actress filming a scene, although I hadn't noticed that before. The same man who had gestured a moment before approaches again. He appears to be the director. No longer alarmed, I glance over at the gentleman lying next to me.

One of the oddest things about dreaming lucidly is that dreaming awareness is single focused; even though I'd watched the director coming toward me a moment earlier, when I looked over at the gentleman lying next to me, I immediately lost awareness of the director.

The act of cognition is different while dreaming than in the wakened state. A thought can appear, and it doesn't automatically follow that the next thought will relate in any way, shape, or form to the first thought, just as an image can be present in a dream, and in the very next moment, it can be gone.

I suspect this has a great deal to do with the solidness of the cohesion held by the dreamer at any given moment in time. There's little sense of sequencing in dreaming. The level of volition the dreamer has at their command factors into the action of the dream for as long as the dreamer can hold the cohesion of the scene in which they find themselves.

Back in the dream, as I look at the gentleman lying next to me in bed, I think, *I'll shout at this guy to see what type of energy he is.* Quickly, I reconnoitered. *No! You're not going to shout at this man lying six inches from your face, silly! You have other choices, you know.* I had enough awareness to recognize that my urge to shout came from reading *The Art of Dreaming*. In the book, Don Juan plays a joke on Castaneda when he instructs him to shout at objects in his dreams so that eventually he would shout at the Tenant in a display of mock authority.[11]

The Tenant is an energetic being, who centuries ago chose to remain in dreaming realms not of this world. For those who choose to do dreaming, the Tenant can become a formidable foe. I was not going to be tricked into doing silly things like yelling at the Tenant while dreaming. However, I could point my finger at objects in the dream to determine foreign energy, which was another technique to develop lucid dreaming more fully.

For instance, looking around carefully, I focus my eyes on the ceramic ware located on the pine shelving on the wall. Pointing covertly at one of the vases (so no one would catch me at what I am doing), I hold my finger steady. Slowly, the vase shimmers and morphs into a vase of slightly different shape, color, and size.

Moving from one vase to another, I point to all of the ceramic objects. *Move slowly, Jessica, so you don't lose it,* I caution myself. Excitement had a way of breaking up dreaming cohesion. *And don't stare at anything for too long, remember?*

Staring at any object while dreaming for too long causes the dreamer to get lost in the detail of that single object. All of us do this in daily reality, and oftentimes don't realize that's what we're doing. Say you have an argument with a friend. After the argument is over and done with, it's tempting to go over and over the conversation to determine how it might have gone differently from your perspective. We begin to perseverate on portions of the conversation we wished to change in the hope of having attained a different outcome. The same perseveration occurs during lucid dreaming and can easily detract us from the purpose for the dreaming itself.

One time while dreaming, I found myself staring at the back of my hands. The veins and wrinkles in the skin, the small freckles, the folds of delicate skin covering each knuckle, and the small pink valleys spanning each digit had fascinated me. I'd spent all of my available energy looking at the back of my hands. I couldn't pull myself away from the detail. Just because I was dreaming lucidly didn't mean that I had the attendant volition to do anything differently than what I found myself doing at the moment I became lucid.

All of the objects I point at in the dreaming bedroom shimmy for a moment, then change shape and color while retaining their original form. In other words, they are exactly what they present themselves to be in the dreaming bedroom. In *The Art of Dreaming,* Don Juan instructs Castaneda that when he points at an object, and it sizzles rather than shimmies, foreign energy is in the dream.[12] This is neither good nor bad, but definitely something to be aware of. It could mean that an inorganic being was a visitor while dreaming.

Covertly, I point at the men lying next to me. Why was it so important that they not suspect I was pointing at them? I don't know. I know that while dreaming in the sleep state, my thinking process isn't the same as when I'm awake. Dozens of times I have come out of dreaming and quizzed myself on what I could have done differently. But that was after my familiar way of being had resumed outside of the dreaming. At that point I was operating from a different cognition than while dreaming. None of the men I am so stealthily pointing at change shape or colors, all of them remain the same, so at that point no foreign energy is present in my dreaming that I am aware of.

Rising from the bed, I get up and walk out the bedroom door. Entering a different room, I see clothing on the bed and recognize it as the wardrobe change needed for the next scene. I wonder how long I can continue pointing at various objects. At the very instant I wonder how long my dreaming will last, the objects around me become blurry and lose their vivid color.

This has happened before. Did asking the question prompt the end of the dreaming or was it a signpost to hold the cohesion in order to continue the dreaming? Again, I don't know. It is one of the reasons I wanted to study with a Nagual. I expected the Nagual to direct me as I developed my dreaming. What I know is that each and every time the thought occurs to me to wonder how long I can continue dreaming, the very next moment the dreaming scene begins to fade and I lose my cohesion, or said another way, my assemblage point moves away from its current location.

I slowly come out of the dream to find myself lying still in my "real" bed, feeling complete awe and wonder. The vividness and clarity of color in dreaming made everyday reality dull and ordinary. I understood why Castaneda loved Dreaming! It was the most curious, fantastic, bizarre experience imaginable. I wanted to spend as much time in dreaming as my awareness would allow. At the same time, I "got" that dreaming was a dangerous place that required vigilance. The danger involved the dreamer getting caught up in the wild experience of dreaming and losing focus on the pivotal act of placing awareness that occurs during the dreaming experience. It would be akin to being seated behind the wheel of a vehicle when you begin to spontaneously visualize being in another location. Termed "highway hypnosis" in your mind you're no longer behind the wheel of your car but in another location. When you realize with a start that "you" are not in the same location as is your physical body, you bring your awareness back to the present moment to avoid getting into an accident. The potential for danger is high when you are in two different locations at one time.

To help the reader understand the allure of dreaming, I'll provide a parallel in daily life. Imagine, at this very moment, someone comes to your front door and offers you a heretofore unimaginable fortune. The amount might be different for each and every person, but it is an amount that you never dreamed of acquiring. There are no strings attached and, as far as you know, you're free to do with the money whatever you want to do with it.

What is unfamiliar and possibly unknown to you is the importance of an attachment to the money that gets developed. Before you quite realize what is happening, the money begins to own you rather than the other way around. Thinking about the money and how to spend it begins to dominate your waking hours and your every decision. You lose a sense of balance in dealing with the money. Before you know it, the money and all the potential connections to be made with it dominate your life. It becomes a cruel and lifeless taskmaster. This is the allure of dreaming for those who practice it. Dreaming is a practice that holds easy ruin for those who overindulge.

July 28

At Kualoa Ranch on Oahu lies a valley that is an ancient wonder of volcanic geology. The sides of the valley are formed by volcanic rock that cascade hundreds and hundreds of feet like emerald-green velvet drapes, the hem of which sweeps perpendicular to the valley floor. The vegetation is every shade of green imaginable: viridian, mantis, and olive, including the green of fruits and vegetables such as lime, apple, and asparagus. The valley narrows to an upside down "v" several miles inland from the ocean and at that apex laps over to continuing folds of vertical cliffs on the opposite side facing Chinaman's Hat, the dollop island where we'd kayaked to the beachside cave months ago.

Hiking trails run like arteries through the valley, but only for those who know their whereabouts, otherwise they are hidden to the newly arrived visitor. Unless the trails are used and groomed continuously, they become overgrown within weeks. Unattended loi (taro) fields dot the flat area near the valley's entrance, as do koi ponds. Cattle have been introduced in the valley and wander quite content near the lands that accordion toward the ocean like a splayed fan. A few campsites have been roughly built, and the remnants of several filming sets still remain, even though movie crews are long gone.

Barbara and I arrived on site in the late afternoon to find the Nagual and a handful of women who have been setting up tents since mid-morning away from previous campsites. Their faces are beet-red from the sun but they don't complain. The weather forecast predicted heavy rainfall for the weekend. In its stead, the sun was a welcome boon. No one was sure how long the unexpected warmth would last, so the ladies had worked tirelessly to get tents, awnings, and camping gear in place.

As the late afternoon turned to evening dusk, we hiked a

small knoll to the right of the kitchen area. As we arrived at the top, we noticed the labyrinth of blue cord laid out vigilantly by Suzanne earlier in the day, nestled in amongst the bur clover, pokeweed, and nettle that covered the mound.

Building labyrinths was Suzanne's deal. She came prepared with the rope and pegs necessary to build the circular maze. Uncertain at the outset as to where to build, Suzanne was pleased the hillock turned out to be the perfect location, serving the same purpose a lighthouse does hanging on an ocean cliffside. Suzanne was eager to show us her handiwork.

One at a time, we walked up to the entrance of the labyrinth, and the Nagual anointed each of us with rose oil and gave each one of us a stone with the name of a spirit animal to guide our actions during the weekend. Inscribed on my stone was the word "Hawk" and alongside it the word "messenger." I was curious about getting Hawk as a spirit guide. I associated Hawk with hunting, keen vision, and flight, rather than messenger. I felt a sense of solemnity as she performed this welcoming act, like accepting the wafer from the priest at mass. Each woman in turn walked the blue web of rope much like walking a spiral staircase laid flat on the ground. Suzanne tells us that the power of the labyrinth builds as people walk it. She instructs us to walk mindfully, not to rush, and to focus our minds on nothing. A premium time to walk is when distractions from anyone else present are at a minimum. I recognized my love of learning new information as Suzanne shared her knowledge of the labyrinth with us. The Nagual invited us to come and walk the labyrinth as often as we liked during the weekend.

For the weekend I was assigned to sleep in a large tent with three other women. Two of the women I knew from Tuesday and Thursday evenings, and one woman was a new acquaintance. Earlier I'd heard chatter about who got assigned with whom in what tent, but I didn't care; as long as I had room to sleep comfortably, I was a happy camper. Close to midnight we arranged our sleeping bags and began to bed down for the night. Sleep came quickly. It seemed as though the long day had started way back the day before. Hours later, I woke to a preternatural light beaming into the tent's central window. I didn't know the origin of the light beam and momentarily wondered if someone were outside the tent with a flashlight, poking around. *Ah,* I remembered, *the moon was full just a few days ago.*

I recognized the slow measured breathing of sleep all around me. No one else was awake. Never had I seen such tensile strength in moonbeams before! They had volume to them, a kind of solidity as though I could mount them and be transported into the starry night. I soaked up the moonbeams and slowly returned to sleep with high expectations for what would transpire over the next two days. Remember, the East on the medicine wheel is the place of co-creation with the Universe in our daily lives. Recognizing the beauty and majesty of the moonbeams and taking in their preternatural essence was a highpoint in the weekend. Never before had I paid such close attention to how nature provided me with sustenance for my spirit and a heartfelt connection with the unspoken.

Early the next morning, I hiked the short path up to the labyrinth. At this point in the weekend, I had no idea how powerfully the labyrinth would soon affect me; I only knew that I liked Suzanne's devotion to the labyrinth and her interest in it drew me to walk it again. Several others were already there but no one was talking. An aura of silence permeated nature's sanctuary on the top of this little hobbit hill. I walked the length of the cobalt cord to the center with a measured pace and returned the way I had come. Next, I scouted out a suitable spot on the grass to sit and meditate. The sun hadn't yet risen above the height of the velvet cliffs, but it wasn't far off as the early morning sky morphed seamlessly from blue into sunshine yellow. A soft wind swirled around me and I greeted it with pleasure.

Meditation acted upon me as I sat in the valley paradise. Peace and serenity surrounded and filled me as I communed with the elements. All was well! The ebb and flow of my life was in pristine balance at this moment, as nature once again filled me with timeless energy. Time ceased to exist as I sat alone in the bosom of the valley on this little knob hill.

The aroma of coffee wafted up the trail, and I joined the group for breakfast. The morning was filled with a group project: to create a collage from magazine cutouts of those experiences that had been pivotal to our lives in the past year. This was a project I had often completed as an art therapist with adolescents in treatment facilities, although many in the morning group had never done it before. After completing the collage, the group shared their self-discoveries with each other. Meanwhile Liz bustled around the makeshift kitchen, preparing the remaining meals for the day.

Liz was the Nagual's partner and, fortunately or not, had thus garnered the position of organizer of outings, collector of funds, cook, and transportation chief. She took her cooking responsibilities seriously; she was a no-nonsense kind of gal. She delegated tasks for those lingering in the area after breakfast. Her directives took on a familiar tone as they had during the previous month's weekend on the Big Island.

"How many of us are here?" she questioned. "Count out that exact number of chicken breasts for tonight.

"Dice these one-quarter inch," she ordered, referring to the potatoes, "no more, no less; understand? Come on! Show me how you do it." There was no room for error, else she would begin to bark and bite, like a drill sergeant on the parade field. "Close that lid on the brown sugar! Who opened it? The moisture will cause it to clump."

I observed that she directed her commands to certain people while never to others. "Didn't I tell you the water isn't hot enough yet? Heat it more." Her attention to people felt predatory. "You didn't give a rat's ass about how you sorted these pinto beans, did you? Look, I found three that needed to be pulled out." When those women complied, she sought them out again.

She began to stay away from me. I knew she could sense my unhappiness at being commanded. Damn! The same thing was happening again. During the last trip I had finally left the kitchen area in abject frustration. Once again I was watching myself and others orient to a commander in the kitchen. There wasn't going to be any camaraderie, no joking and laughing, no playful antics as we all joined hands in making our meal together.

As at the past weekend retreat when I returned to eat, there was no pleasure in the meal. I was uneasy. Others were uneasy. However, there was no complaint about the food; it was excellent in every way. But it came at a price; and for the price demanded, I would rather pay for the meal at a restaurant and be done with a cook barking orders like a Gatling gun.

A hike was scheduled for the afternoon to the far end of the valley. The Nagual didn't mention the purpose for the hike, and so I assumed she intended for the experience itself to be our teacher. The hike would also be a chance to get away from Liz. She'd stay behind to begin preparation for the evening meal. Before I recognized what was happening, I was organizing my weekend experience around Liz and her drill sergeant commands. Damn that woman! I wasn't the only one to be impacted by Liz's dominating manner; I could see and hear the tension from the other apprentices, too.

We loaded into a van that took us closer to the outset of our hike. For several hours, we navigated the trail up the jungle ascent. I heard complaints murmured about the length of time the hike was taking and the precarious conditions of the trail. Just as building labyrinths was Suzanne's "thing," an immense source of happiness to her, hiking was pure pleasure for me. Scrambling up and down slippery slopes, grasping onto the moldy twine knotted to random trees in order to pull ourselves further up the trail, seeing delicate magic mushrooms and wild orchids growing at our feet, finding the last of the edible summer guava, and smelling the humus-rich soil – I reveled in these things.

I empathized with those women who struggled during the hike. I struggled with being around Liz; they appeared to handle her micromanaging better than I was able to. I loved every moment of the four-hour-long hike; their discomfort could easily be heard by the weary comments muttered under their breaths.

"Hook into the energy lines as we walk up this grade. They will give you a boost," the Nagual suggested. Again, the Nagual was using the natural environment for teaching. The earth was a conduit for energy and a boon to knowledge, yet how many of the apprentices knew to tap into her resources? To view the hike as an exercise in endurance, sweat, and physical fatigue was to miss what it had to offer. I was reminded of the Nagual's teaching on filter systems months ago. Many of the women engaged in the collage activity as though a structured lesson was preferable to a teaching from a natural setting. The natural setting was what the Nagual was good at utilizing. I was grateful for her focus on the unstructured, organic teachings rather than the formal, organized activities such as the collage offered earlier that morning.

I concentrated on walking in silence and watching each step as I pulled myself along the twine tied to trees to help hikers up the trail. There was no fear of snakes in Hawaii, as there was in Southern California. We only needed to watch for the incessant mosquitoes that landed quietly and bit viciously, which I'd learned the hard way upon first arriving in Hawaii. One mosquito bite could leave a nasty lump, soreness, heat, and droning pain for a month. I was acclimating though; they bit me less often and didn't leave nearly the same size welt as when I'd arrived the previous fall.

As we returned up the grade to cross the escarpment back to the valley we'd come from two hours earlier, I stopped. Suddenly, I called out to the Nagual, "Hey! One valley feels feminine and the other feels masculine." The change in energy between the two had been as distinct as walking through a doorway.

"You used gender to describe the change in energy that you feel from one valley to the next," the Nagual explained. "Someone else might describe it differently using descriptors unique to their life experience." I was amazed at the energy I experienced during the hike regardless of how I'd described it to the Nagual. Nothing could have prepared me for the change in the energy between the two valleys beyond experiencing it for myself. The ramifications for me were intriguing: energy is evident everywhere, and as human beings who respond to the energy around us we make choices as to how to interact with that energy. I remembered Bruce telling me that, "There are only two options for what to do with the energy we feel. Energy either expands our being or depletes it." I chose to take in the heterogeneous energy I felt while in both valleys. We continued hiking down the slope and soon arrived back at the van that returned us to our campsite.

The following morning I paused at the entrance to the labyrinth. The morning sun was on the cusp of rising, wrestling its way through gunmetal-gray clouds. Rain had been falling steadily through the wee hours of the morning, and the hardy grasses and weeds scattered throughout the labyrinth were bowed from its weight. For the moment, the rain was on break, and I was a solitary figure amidst the valley, the clouds, the wind, the labyrinth, and the moist earth. Engrossed, I stepped into the circle and began walking mindfully. Transcendence. The peace at being there, still and alone, was tremendous.

My thoughts were nowhere, still and at rest. The storeroom of my mind was empty. Out of the blue a thought came that the

Nagual was compromised as a Nagual by her relationship with Liz. I knew, without knowing how I knew, that the Nagual expended a tremendous amount of energy on her relationship with Liz and that expenditure compromised the amount of energy she had for her apprentices, almost as though she was on automatic pilot when with us. This was the level of clarity that walking a labyrinth can bring. The certainty of the knowledge was without any doubt.

Immediately, I wondered if the Nagual knew. *Yes,* my intuition confirmed, *she knows but prefers not to know. She will know it more fully if she wants to.* This knowledge explained for me the source of tension I experienced during monthly activities with the Nagual. My sense that Liz was oftentimes at odds with both the Nagual and the Nagual's teachings was confirmed in the clarity provided by walking the labyrinth, though receiving this clarity felt like Pandora wishing desperately she hadn't lifted the lid off the treasure box. Then I remembered that Power coming in the form of knowledge doesn't need to be shared unless the opportunity arises to do so. At the moment, it didn't occur to me that the opportunity to speak would soon be at my doorstep.

Our camping area was set up on several levels with a dirt road that connected to all of them. The dirt road was full of ruts and potholes that would challenge most any respectable vehicle. The top level was where the labyrinth sat. Down a sharp incline, negotiable only on foot and leaning to the right, was the kitchen area. The dirt road was in the shape of a descending letter "S," and further down was the Nagual's tent. At the end, or the beginning, depending on which direction you were traveling, was an open area where three or four tents were set up to provide sleeping shelters for the rest of the participants during the weekend.

After breakfast that second morning, Liz drove her truck up the road in order to begin loading her gear. As she turned the truck to head up the hill, making a three-point turn, she found herself on an incline with the bed of the truck on the downward slope. The back end of the truck had slipped off the dirt road and the rear tires were in soft dirt. At this juncture, she was unable to move the truck, its weight not heavy enough or traction strong enough to complete the turn. Spinning the tires in the soft dirt only served to make the situation worse, and the truck was unable to move one inch. The truck… was stuck.

Everyone rallied around. First, everyone was directed to get into the bed of the truck, hoping our combined weight would provide the truck with traction. No help. "Everybody out!" hollered the Nagual.

Second, another vehicle was tied to the truck as a tow. The rope broke. The truck stayed put. Opinions and suggestions were flying like shrapnel. People got heated and anger pierced the air like loose arrows. "She did this last time, too; can't she manage this truck?" a participant complained.

Standing alongside the truck, I was in the throes of indecision. How long did I want to stay in the fray? Had I made myself available to assist for long enough? This tension between Liz and the Nagual often arose in a group setting. What was the best possible course of action in the moment?

Without second-guessing, I made my decision. I walked away. I walked up the hill and sat down at the picnic table out of view of the others. Within a few minutes others joined me; I suspected they also were frustrated at the situation and considered that walking away was their best option. We continued to hear the shouts and exclamations as the others redoubled the rope, retied the two vehicles together and, with shouts of victory, coaxed the truck back onto the road.

Soon I found myself taking down the tent and packing camping gear along with everyone else. After attending to our belongings, the group convened one last time at the picnic table in the kitchen area.

"Any thoughts, feelings, or comments about the weekend?"

the Nagual asked, glancing around at everyone.

Vicky spoke up first. Vicky didn't attend the weekly meetings often; in fact, I had had minimal interaction with her in the previous six months. "I have some thoughts, but I don't know if this is the right time to bring them up," she said. Vicky was asking permission to have a voice, I thought ruefully. The air was pregnant with tension, although I suspected it had something more to do with Liz and her truck than it did with Vicky lacking confidence to share her opinion. No one said a word. "Maybe now's not the time then," Vicky backed down, convinced she had nothing worthwhile to say.

When the Nagual asked for our thoughts, feelings, and comments, I suddenly knew why I'd received Hawk, the messenger. I spoke up immediately before I lost my own confidence. The message was clear even though I hadn't given any thought to Hawk throughout the weekend. It wasn't an easy message. Quickly I decided that saying something positive first would help ease the potential for awkwardness.

"I loved the labyrinth. It was a highpoint of the weekend for me. Walking it has been amazing. Suzanne, thank you for your knowledge of the labyrinth and for making it available for us."

"As to the hike yesterday, Katie, thank you for being the contact allowing us to be here and for knowing the trails. We wouldn't have gotten half as far without you knowing where those hidden trails were."

Then I turned to Liz and gave her direct eye contact so she would know I was speaking to her, because it was a message that was difficult to give. "I received the Hawk as my spirit helper this weekend," I began. "The Hawk stands for messenger."

"I don't do well being barked at when I'm asked to help prepare meals. Your stern tone sets up such a negative experience for me." This portion of the message from Hawk raised hair on the back of my neck. No wonder fear and aggression went hand-in-hand. The hawk was an assertive, forceful image. The same things would never have been said had my spirit animal been a dove. I stopped. I turned to the Nagual and looked directly into her eyes, those eyes that took no quarter. I forged on through my fear.

"I walked the labyrinth often this weekend and it gave me an amazing sense of clarity. Although the clarity I received was about an unexpected topic." I paused and then said quickly, "I think the constant friction between you and Liz compromises the energy work that can be done while you are with your apprentices."

The silence in the group was ominous, like the heavy rainclouds that had hung in the sky over the better portion of the weekend. But I had heard enough from the other apprentices to know that the relationship between the Nagual and her partner weighed heavy on others, too, not just on me. Speaking up was like announcing an elephant in the room. It had become part of the group norm to ignore and overlook these instances that occurred frequently when the Nagual and Liz were together in the group.

The Nagual's blue eyes were sharp, a knife puncturing a sausage, innards oozing through the slice in the membrane. "My spirit helper was the bat," she countered. Our eyes locked. Hers spoke volumes. We held the tension, two wrestlers in a lockout, sweaty, fierce, muscles strained to their maximum.

"For those of you who want to go the way of the shaman, the only way to do it is to be an apprentice. The message of the bat is death and rebirth as is the experience of the shaman. And the apprentice's buttons will be pushed; that is part of the experience. Your job is not to react emotionally." Our eyes remained locked in the tension between us.

No one said a word. Gripping silence held us for a moment, and then I couldn't hold the strain a second longer. I looked away. The Nagual chose to sidestep the issue I had addressed and to view it as an emotional reaction on my part. Rather than own her contribution to the conflict she brought to the group as a result of her relationship with her partner, she pointed the finger of accusation at me. Several apprentices spoke hesitantly trying to bridge the gaping tension, but the meeting petered to a close within minutes. There wasn't enough collective energy to keep a discussion going. The group disbanded as we began to gather our belongings in order to go home.

Several apprentices approached me. "Thank you," they said gratefully, "for speaking up. If you hadn't said what you did, I would have." I was touched by their disclosure. I wasn't the only one to be impacted by the events as they had unfolded throughout the weekend.

Part Four: South

– The direction of innocence and trust in ourselves, the place of growth and maturity into who we are. It is the direction of shedding energies from the past, the place of the heart, a place of abundance and passion.

The sun rises to its apex in the fullness of summer days and brings with it the ripeness of the season and, in addition, our hearts into abundance.

August 25

The monthly full moon ceremony came and went. I did not attend.

As a therapist with clients that scheduled weekly appointments, I tracked my clients' attendance easily. When a client came consistently and then began to miss random appointments, there was usually a reason. The therapist's job, if the therapist wants to track the coming and going of the clients as an element of therapy, is to use that tracking as a point of discussion: "Are we on target? Are we looking at the issues that are important to you? Do we need to redirect?"

It's easy to track missed sessions around the Christmas season, and easy to track missed sessions in months with five weeks. Those cancellations often deal with financial issues. It's easy to track missed sessions after having a session in which thorny issues were discussed; those cancellations most often pertained to vulnerability.

There is lots of theory and discussion about the topic of regularity and consistency in therapy sessions in the trade. Some therapists use it as a therapeutic issue; others do not. I was a therapist who thought it useful to watch for patterns and to offer discussion once those patterns developed.

Apparently, the Nagual was also aware of the comings and goings of the apprentices; although up to that point, I'd not missed one event, appointment, or activity.

On this morning I went to my weekly appointment with the Nagual for her massage. At the completion of the massage, the Nagual asked if I had a few moments to speak with her. I nodded. I had time.

"I was out and about dreaming the other night," she began. "When I came to you, you acted hesitant to come along, almost as though you were pushing me away. I noticed your resistance," the Nagual explained.

Immediately, the term "resistance" put me off. *How about finding out the circumstances first before labeling me "resistant,"* I thought. And how could I forget that the last direct interaction we had the month before during the weekend campout was when I had shared that her relationship with her partner compromised her work as a Nagual. But then again, my dreaming had stopped. I couldn't disagree on that fact. So maybe this was what she was picking up on.

"My dreaming has changed," I said, my tone perplexed. "Remember, last month when I called you about Carlos Castaneda's second gate of dreaming in his book, *The Art of Dreaming*? Since then I've not dreamed at all. My dreaming has come to a screeching halt," I lamented.

"That's due to fear," she announced plainly.

Then why hadn't she used the term "fear" rather than "resistance"? I thought. Resistance implied that I was being willful and disobedient.

I sighed. How could I tell the Nagual that I found it very difficult to discuss anything with her? Was it my lack of confidence, or was it the expectations I had for her as the Nagual that held me back from having an easy and authentic conversation with her? Was it her choice of words, her role as an authority figure, or her brusqueness when she spoke with me? I sighed feeling stymied yet one more time. I hadn't been able to decipher what rang true on any consistent basis.

"You didn't attend the full moon ceremony," the Nagual continued. More often than not, the Nagual made statements rather than asked questions.

"No, I didn't. Scheduled ceremony doesn't have much appeal for me," I stated plainly, not willing to give a trumped-up excuse. "I find that I don't want to come to the monthly Sunday meetings either," I confessed, already feeling a twinge of guilt for not wanting to attend the next one on Sunday.

"That's exactly when you should come." The Nagual smiled as though the cat just swallowed the canary. Her belief was that resistance always comes before a breakthrough.

And how could I tell the Nagual that it felt uncomfortable at the Sunday "open" meetings that she always expected "testimonials" from her apprentices during the introductory time? This was an unspoken prompt I observed consistently for the past six months. As if on cue during a Sunday gathering an apprentice would speak up and share their continuing interest in studying with the Nagual, a sales pitch through and through.

"I notice you don't interact much with the others," the Nagual stated, positing another one of her non-queries. *Where is this line of reasoning going?* I wondered. It had been a long time since the Nagual had spoken to me personally. Her comments felt as though she'd been stockpiling observations, and they were all coming at me at once – rat-a-tat-tat-tat. I couldn't think how to respond.

"You know," I said, "I've made several gestures to some of the other women for friendship, but it really hasn't gone anywhere." Where was she leading me with these questions that had no question mark?

"I suggest you look at the issues of intimacy," she continued, then abruptly switched her line of questioning.

"How did you come to study the Toltec path?"

Stunned, I stood with my mouth open. The Nagual had never asked me anything about myself, not even in her office the day I asked about healing my tooth when I'd first met her. I hadn't seen the question coming; it wasn't information the Nagual had ever shown interest in before. She had never seemed much interested in an apprentice's backstory. Yet I had always been eager to tell her. Regardless of not knowing where the question had come from or why it showed up at this odd juncture in our relationship, I wanted the Nagual to know me better.

I shared about my initial meeting with a psychologist who

had given Castaneda's first book, *The Teachings of Don Juan: A Yaqui Way of Knowledge*,[13] as a reading assignment to his clients lost in the morass of hallucinogenic drugs. Those clients included my daughter, and out of curiosity, when the psychologist advised that my daughter read the book, I read it also.

I told her about being a pastor's wife and the dawning awareness, after years of being devoted to the church, that I was trapped in a world of religious dogma. I shared my passion for gaining freedom from all of the ways that boxed me in psychologically, spiritually, and ideologically. The Toltec path offered perceptual freedom in a way I'd never known before. From the moment I'd begun reading Castaneda's books, I had embraced his worldview.

Pausing, I brought myself back to the present. "I'm not a person who enjoys chitchat; I'm direct," I stated. "More direct than is good for me much of the time. It doesn't always bode well for easy friendships. The reason I'm with you is to gain growth on this path."

The Nagual chuckled, "If you'll notice, I'm not one to do much chitchatting either. Allow yourself to broaden your boundaries. Go down to the mall, sit and watch people, expand your energy. Come early and stay late at the meetings. Become friends with the others."

As I drove home, turmoil turned my stomach with as much speed as the tires spinning on their axles. I was not a student of the Nagual in order to resolve psychological issues, that much I knew. I had been with her long enough to observe those topics that were important to her, and developing friendships hadn't been one of them until now. But still, what was my internal racket about? It took the forty-five minute drive home to organize my feeling of chaos.

First, I noted my overreaction. It bothered me that the Nagual honed in on the issue of intimacy. I had come to her to gain guidance on the Toltec path, but if the shoe of intimacy was a fit,

I ought to wear it, to let go of defending myself and change my interactions with the other apprentices.

Second, I wondered about the concept of "no out there." This was a term that the Nagual used but did it apply to her? I wasn't bothered or troubled by a lack of interaction with my peers. From my perspective, our interactions were at a level that felt comfortable for the circumstance we found ourselves in. I was interested in a student/teacher relationship with the Nagual, not with the other apprentices, but in this instance the Nagual was pointing the intimacy finger at me.

Third, how did the conversation get from, "You were resistant when I saw you in dreaming," to, "You have intimacy issues"?" I accepted the premise that she could appear in my dreams. I also knew the reality that my dreaming had come to an abrupt stop. What I couldn't fathom was how the Nagual had put non-dreaming side by side with lack of intimacy.

Fourth, I hadn't been able to say these very things to her face to face while standing in her kitchen forty minutes earlier. Often, when I spoke up too soon in a conversation with a potential for conflict, I would say something I'd end up regretting. Hadn't it happened often enough during discussions on Tuesday and Thursday evenings? But if I didn't speak up, the opportunity to respond was lost. I was caught in the jaws of a dilemma.

I came to the Nagual to achieve freedom, not to discover how to develop friendships. Freedom meant gaining a point of view in daily life free from preconceived ideas, values, beliefs, and emotions. I came to the Nagual in order to move into the experience of non-duality rather than to be loaded down with muddy filter systems from ideological, religious, and psychological beliefs. I wasn't a novice at making friends and developing intimate relationships. I was a novice at practicing a Toltec lifestyle – unless making friends, opening up dreaming, and being more intimate *was* a Toltec lifestyle as the Nagual was indicating. If that were the case, I was sorely lost or traveling with the wrong roadmap. Most importantly, I wasn't able to communicate with the Nagual in a manner that would clear up any of my confusion. Not attending the moon ceremony was a missed appointment, and I was on the way to missing a second. What change was adrift in this unruly heart?

August 27

Tuesday evening Crow flew in the window and hopped along the length of my legs as I lay on the carpet during the evening's meditation. Hmm, that's where the phrase "crow hop" comes from, I mused. Jumping onto my stomach, Crow stood looking at me with its head cocked to one side. I greeted the grow (a typo – I meant to type "crow" – I never realized how many omens come through the computer keyboard). Telepathically, its message was clear: "Be aware, next month is big. A *lot* will be going on." And that was it. The meditation was over. Crow was gone.

Thursday evening, flying in the window for the third time in a year, the Crow arrived again during the evening meditation. "Commit to finishing your book by year's end," came its voice in my mind. Crow's tone was imperative, allowing no argument. I had been working on a manuscript since coming to Hawaii; but due to long hours at work, it had been hit and miss the entire time. Consistently, I'd found that my writing time ended up being squeezed into the end of the day. This was the first time Crow had shown cognizance of my writing. Weird.

Often I was tired and preoccupied after a full day at the agency. More often than not, when I sat down at the computer in the late evenings, the writing became a chore I began to avoid. With a work schedule that ballooned to over fifty hours a week, committing to regular writing was becoming an impossible feat of time management. "Leaving the Nagual would give you evenings and weekends for your writing," the Crow suggested offhandedly. "You'd have a full four month's time to focus on your writing," the Crow spelled out the advantage of no longer attending Tuesday and Thursday evenings, along with not attending the weekend activities, for the remainder of the year.

My reaction to Crow's proposal was swift: heart palpitation, heat radiating up through my torso into my head, and tears swelling underneath my eyelids. No! No! I was on board with the Nagual for the long haul. Not once had my intermittent unhappiness in my relationship with the Nagual put the apprenticeship itself into question. In my heart, my commitment to the apprenticeship spanned the three or four years I intended to live in Hawaii. My prototype for the time an apprenticeship lasted came from knowing that Carlos Castaneda's apprenticeship with Don Juan lasted ten years, and the Nagual's own apprenticeship had lasted three years. An apprenticeship of a year was merely a beginning. Besides, Crow hadn't indicated the apprenticeship was over, rather that I was to take a break for several months.

My concerns, complaints, and questions regarding my time with the Nagual were all viewed as "fodder for the mill," as a therapist would say; simply the give and take in any evolving, ongoing relationship. Things would smooth out. We would stretch and grow and learn from each other, and both of us would be better for it in the end. My commitment was solid, backed by the unseen Intent that had brought me there.

Quietly, I slipped out after the meditation was over. *What will the Nagual think?* I wondered. *Will she think I'm avoiding intimacy? Will she think I'm insisting on doing things my way?* My questions covered both events: leaving immediately after the meditation was over that evening, and leaving the apprenticeship at the end of the year if even for a short time. But regardless of what the Nagual might think, my intention was to follow Crow's directive. Crow was not a casual visitor.

A crow flying through the window and coming to me during a meditation was a big deal, as big as a coyote running across the horizon in Carlos Castaneda's world. As big as completing a Life Book had been for the Nagual during her apprenticeship. I wasn't the only apprentice to speak of visitations during the meditations, but I had been curious about the meaning those visitations held for the other apprentices. Others also spoke of dream images, just as I did.

What was the reason the other apprentices treated those images as though they were not corporeal, as though they were fanciful events that were fun to indulge in but not to take seriously? What was the point of having dreams and meditations and then treating them as though they were elements of the subconscious? In one sense that's what they are; however, time and again that definition only seems to give license to treat the experience as a chimera, a waft of light particles forming an image that was metaphorical at best. To treat them as though energy from a different reality was present and in communication with me held me responsible to act on the message.

I was moving into the lesson of the South on the medicine wheel, a time of trusting in my own growth and maturity. Knowledge was at my doorstep during my meditation travels, and I was responsible to use that knowledge in my daily life. Lessons were meant to be acted upon, not merely listened to. That's what non-duality was all about: bringing together the disparate events in our lives into a unified, energetic whole as we let go of past energies at the same time.

September 3

Barbara from our group had a home business as a psychic. A telephone call later and we'd agreed to exchange our services. I was to give her a massage and she would give me a reading. My effort was a follow-through on the Nagual's suggestion that I develop friendships with others in the group.

The next day Barbara called to cancel our appointment. She was tired from doing readings all day. She agreed that some time in the future we could reschedule our exchange, but she didn't suggest an alternative date to put on the calendar. I suggested we schedule for the following week.

"It's really difficult for me to schedule that far in advance. My regular clients call at odd times and I want to be fully available for them whenever they call," she explained. Our call came to an end, and within a few minutes my phone rang.

A friend from New Mexico, Catherine, whom I hadn't spoken with for a long while, was on the phone. We had met at that workshop three years prior in Montana, the same time that I had dreamed for the South direction and had a vision of my life that involved a bear, bear scat, and a river. We hadn't spoken with each other since my move to Hawaii. Her eager voice after the unexpected turndown from Barbara felt like a Starbuck latte, warm and enticing. I talked and talked, of the good, the bad, and the ugly in my experience with the Nagual. There was no prohibition in my comments. I didn't hold back and my voice revealed a pent-up frustration that startled me as I heard it.

Was this interruption in my apprenticeship with the Nagual leading to the end of my apprenticeship? She was the reason I'd gone to Hawaii in the first place! I hadn't seen this coming, this change in direction related to my apprenticeship. Without even knowing it, I had come to the conclusion that because I was there, I would study with the Nagual for the entire time I was in

Hawaii, maximize what she had to offer. I was startled at how my assumptions and expectations had taken shape with no room for alteration.

Funny how I'd assumed that a "good" thing was a forever thing, and following in lockstep with that idea had been the assumption that anything short-term was a "bad" thing. Longer was better for an apprenticeship and shorter was suspect.

In the midst of my ardent explanations to Catherine, the phone signaled another call coming through. I switched over to catch the call. Barbara was asking for a ride to class later in the evening. We settled on a time for pickup, and I switched the call back over to New Mexico. *Odd timing,* I thought. *Why didn't she ask me for a ride during our earlier conversation?*

My conversation with Catherine concluded. A boon to my wilted sense of purpose, my friend had called at such a peculiar time, when I had needed it most. Synchronistically, she'd called at a time when a fresh perspective was a reprieve from my thoughts that were beginning to spin out of control.

The Nagual would call it "seeking an ally," I thought contritely. The act of joining with another energy often supported a particular, sometimes tainted, point of view. Was I pulling people into my point of view to support my perspective, or was I experiencing the moment at hand with freedom from misconceptions? The telephone rang again.

Answering it, I heard Barbara's voice once more. She no longer needed a ride that evening. "Thanks so much anyway," she said; her car was available after all. She'd see me later that night.

For the meditation that evening, the Nagual paired everyone with a partner. Our task was to feel the other person's energy. The Nagual partnered me with Barbara. I smiled at being partnered with her; it was a synchronicity hard to miss. We seated ourselves on the carpet facing each other, and Barbara took my hand into her own. Closing her eyes, she sat in stillness for several minutes and finally began to share her experience.

"Your energy feels quiet, like there is minimal movement going on, almost as though it's closing down," she murmured, as though she was still assessing and searching for an accurate description of the pulse she felt through my hands.

"I'm tired," I responded, nondescriptive in my response because I wanted to hear anything else she had to say without frontloading her with information. I wondered how much she could read from my facial features and body language. Quietly, I waited.

"You're going to leave the group," Barbara announced, as though new information had just been relayed through the energy channels being exchanged through our hands. She looked at me inquisitively.

I stared at her, mouth open and eyes wide. I was impressed. Not even I knew I was leaving the group – well, I had suspected I'd be leaving for a short while – but not for good. Crow had only indicated a break in the apprenticeship, not leaving it altogether.

Quickly I told her the reading was accurate as far as I knew. I told her that I was leaving the Nagual and the group in order to complete the manuscript I had been working on by the end of the year. As I told Barbara the reason I was leaving, I felt like an informer passing on information that could be construed as a betrayal. I glanced around the room to locate the Nagual. Could she hear our conversation? I was speaking behind my own back. I couldn't believe what I heard myself saying. The words were not mine; they belonged to Crow. I wanted to blame him for how they sounded. Saying them felt stiff, like I was wearing a pair of hiking boots for the first time. I wondered how those same words would sound when I said them to the Nagual.

"Guess I got my reading," I whispered into Barbara's ear.

September 4

The details of a dream were fresh on my mind as I awoke. I had gotten into bed the night before and lay there very still. Positioned at the end of the bed, the fan flowed over me and lifted the sheet, causing a fine ripple to dance along my spine. As I placed my attention in the center of my back where I felt the soft slap, slap, slap of the sheet, I realized that the air was no longer coming from the sheets rippled by the fan. The sensation changed into a weight that leaned into the crook of my back. Since my dreaming had stopped for the past month, I was excited to be dreaming lucidly! The weight belonged to the Cat. He was back as a messenger.

Be still so you won't be smothered! I say, not to Cat but to myself. I wait without moving a muscle, my body taut from the flow of Power coming from the presence of Cat. *Trust your body to respond.* Cat nuzzles again and again against my back, smooth and sensual, and I lie still, feeling deep pleasure. Soon I enter more fully into the dreaming state.

In the dream, I am in my own home. The sleek, black Cat roams the house, familiar with the layout of the place. I scoop Cat into my arms and carry him outdoors to the lanai. Cat turns without so much as a glance in my direction and walks straight back through the sliding glass doors into the house. Another creature, an elongated Cat, slinking low-to-the-ground with tawny colored fur, is also in the house. The eyes are alive, crazy alive! Here is the origin of the Power I sensed! I pick the Cat up, "So *you're* really the Power here," I accuse. A huge Cheshire smile spreads across Cat's face.

I didn't understand the meaning of the dream; and I didn't understand my immediate urge to speak with the Nagual, but it was time to speak with her about what Crow had informed me about during the meditation three weeks ago. The dream gave me a sense of urgency to call. I didn't try to figure out what the dream might mean or to analyze it; I simply knew it was time to speak with the Nagual. Nervous, I dialed her number. My breathing bounced off the cell phone held at my mouth, as I listened to the ring on the other end. The distance between the cell phone in my hand and the ring on the other end was a vast no-man's land, and I was momentarily lost in its dry, torpid wasteland.

"Hello," the Nagual answered. I was relieved when she answered her phone – how could I possibly leave this kind of message if she hadn't answered the phone?

"Hi, this is Jessica," I said. "The reason I'm calling is to tell you, uh, that I'm going to concentrate on finishing my book manuscript for the next couple of months, and in order to give myself the time I need to do that, I won't be coming to class any longer." My mouth was as dry as that no-man's land between us.

"Okay," the Nagual responded, without inflection in voice or tone.

"I'll plan on doing your massage for the next two weeks, and I'd like to attend the hike on Saturday, if that's alright."

"Sounds good," she replied, and that was it; the conversation was over. No more explanation or offer of further conversation came from either one of us. The conversation had lasted thirty seconds at most. I had been prepared to explain, to tell her what the Crow had said. I wanted her to help me flush out more about what was happening between us. I wanted her to say, "Jessica, I realize we had a difficult conversation at the Ranch when we were there a month ago. I hope this decision to leave isn't related to that conversation, and that your leaving is only temporary." I had been prepared to have a longer conversation. Neither one happened.

What had I wanted to happen? What did I want… from her?

I stood in the hallway staring at the phone cradled in the palm of my hand. I suddenly knew what I wanted, and I also knew with absolute certainty that what I wanted I wasn't going to get from the Nagual. I wanted her to express some kind of feeling in response to my leaving – concern, curiosity, dismay, disappointment – anything that would tell me she valued me as her apprentice and that she was invested in the relationship between us.

Even though it may have looked all along as though I'd been half-in/half-out the door while I attended everything, and even if I appeared unwilling to make friends and questioned so much of what the Nagual did and said, more than anything in the world I had devoted myself to being her apprentice. My commitment to being an apprentice had been for the long haul.

Standing frozen in space and staring blankly at the mute phone in my hand, a veil fell away, the onion layer called "belief" that circles the earth's orbit at the same time it spins in the mind, and I knew that what I wanted with all of my heart and soul was to surrender and abandon myself to a teacher – a teacher who knew what I didn't know, a teacher who was the only route to gain my freedom. The Nagual's response to my efforts had been either an unwillingness or an inability to acknowledge my commitment and, yes, even my confusion about being her apprentice. Not that she should have, I hasten to add. But that's what I wanted her to do!

It's when I find myself incapable that I must find a hero, but I didn't know that then. I wanted an external person to do what I needed to do for myself. But hero worship devalues the self, and what I needed was to claim my own sense of leadership and ownership for my life, just as the South direction had been calling me to do. However, the only thing I knew at that moment was despair – deep, dark, trembling despair – because I couldn't connect with the Nagual.

For months I had tried to remove myself from the emotional layer of what occurred at the evening meetings, all the while not knowing that I was hooked in at the emotional level of acceptance, approval, and longing. I wanted the Nagual to see me, to see that I wasn't like other apprentices who were halfhearted and flaccid, to see that I was committed, capable, and able to go the distance. Thirty seconds of telephone contact had ripped that artery wide open, the very vein leading to the heart of the matter. I was leaving and her response was, "Okay, sounds good."

September 6

My yoga practice had been choked off. I noticed it that morning. My yoga mat lay parallel alongside my bed. No other space was suitable to practice yoga in the small duplex where we lived except for that area, which was no larger than the mat itself. The bedroom wall was, at the most, eighteen inches on one side of the mat, and my bed was the same distance on the opposite side.

I hadn't noticed until that morning, but I was doing poses that didn't require my legs and arms to be extended beyond the mat. In effect, I had limited the poses I could practice due to the space I was in. There was room to do Downward Dog, but there was no room to do Standing Spread Leg Forward Fold unless I wanted to face plant into the mattress. That morning, I eased myself onto the mat and noticed for the first time that the area was too small and smothering. It felt like being zipped into a mummy bag with no wiggle room.

The Nagual's lecture the evening before had sounded similar to my yoga practice that morning. What she had said was limiting rather than expansive. I had been reminded once again of "no out there." Whatever was occurring in one area of my life would be reflected in other areas. The Nagual had boxed in the definition of intimacy. "Intimacy opens the door to freedom," she'd said. I was listening to the lecture but had somehow missed the segue into intimacy. Barbara hadn't missed it though, and the tail end of her comment was loud and clear… "Then I discovered that I was trying to gain personal freedom without intimacy." I was uncomfortable with her terminology. She was mimicking the Nagual, and what was worse, she didn't even know it.

Hearing the Nagual connect intimacy with freedom was like pointing a finger at the moon: the beauty and mystery of the moon was missed if you looked only at the pointing finger. Freedom was hanging in the sky – full, beautiful, hauntingly close – but intimacy was the finger, merely pointing.

The previous year, when the Nagual had first used the term "love," it was not a term I had been familiar with in the context of the Toltec path. Now she was using the term "intimacy," and that term also was foreign to me in the context of journeying on a Toltec path. At hearing Barbara's next statement, I turned squeamish: "I realized that I needed to explore my intimacy issues before I could gain freedom."

If I could've, I would've screamed.

These women have agreed with the Nagual that her definition of freedom was their definition of freedom! They were reciting the alphabet in a singsong voice just as does a kindergarten child as though they knew the English language when they were merely memorizing a sequence of letters, words, sentences, and paragraphs during their first year in school. They were letting the Nagual do their thinking for them. They were staring at the finger pointing to the moon.

Oh God! Have I been doing the same thing? I wondered.

Vicky spoke about her unhappiness at the weekend retreat in the valley a month ago. The Nagual reminded her, "I've seen over time that you bail again and again when the going gets tough." Vicky didn't say another word. Once again she gave her opinion over to the Nagual.

"Yeah, you're right," she said resignedly. Then the Nagual reiterated to Vicky one of her maxims: "When you want to quit, you're just on the verge of a breakthrough."

Every time the Nagual defined a portion of the Toltec path, I felt intensely compelled to redefine it for myself. Rather than swallow whole what the Nagual was saying, I needed to take it in, chew it for a while, and then swallow. Repeating back verbatim was suspect to me. There was something missing in rote learning. Maybe it was spirit. I was hearing the letter of the law but missing the spirit of that same law.

Once, while facilitating art therapy for adolescents at a crisis shelter, I used still life for one of the art projects. Taking two or three objects, I arranged them in the center of the table, provided pencils and paper, and instructed the kids to draw what they saw. More often than not, they drew what they *thought* they saw, never once looking at the lines, shading, and shape of the objects placed before them. Instead, they would draw their internalized image of what the object looked like.

A stuffed rabbit was my favorite. Instead of drawing the lop-eared, button-eyed, bow tie askance furry animal sitting before them, they drew a stylized version of what a rabbit looked like in cartoons or videos.

A yoga practice that had outgrown its space.

A rabbit occupying the mind rather than an art table.

My apprenticeship was changing at a pace quicker than I could keep up.

September 7

Parking our cars along the road on the east side of the island, the group gathered to wait for two more people to arrive before leaving for the day's hike. Some people had hiked this area before, for others it was their first time; but all of us knew it was the Nagual's favorite spot on the island. I was eager to find out why. The hike followed the cliffside along the ocean, and hiking the lava boulders could be a challenge for those who didn't fancy hiking as a fun thing to do.

While we waited for everyone to arrive, the Nagual asked, "What's your focus for the day?" In her usual teaching style, the Nagual provided the time and location for a weekend activity and expected the apprentice and the experience itself to provide the purpose for the event. I had come to appreciate the Nagual teaching in this manner during weekend activities. Doing so put the responsibility for the experience squarely on the shoulders of each apprentice, so before leaving the house that morning, I had pulled two animal cards from Jamie Sams' *Medicine Cards*.[14] The card deck had sat on the shelf for the past few years, belonging to a period of time when I had been involved in a monthly sweat lodge. Before entering the sweat lodge, we'd pull a card as a means of focusing our Intent. With that sense of timing that permeates non-duality in which things happen at exactly the "right" time, I'd dusted them off early in the morning and pulled two cards from the deck of fifty-some animals.

The first animal, Armadillo, represented boundaries. The card read: "What a gift it is to set your boundaries so that harmful words or intentions just roll off. Your lesson is in setting up what you are willing to experience."[15]

The second animal, Badger, represented aggressiveness: "If Badger is a part of your medicine, you are quick to express your feelings, and you do not care what the consequences are."[16]

Ugh! I hadn't liked the descriptions of either one! Who did Armadillo and Badger represent? What was going to happen that day to push boundaries and set up unusual consequences? But I trusted the cards and could only wait to see how their messages played out. As I stood amidst the group of apprentices, and the Nagual asked for our Intent for the day, the animal names popped from my mouth hot and bothered like kernels of corn in heated oil. Without fail the cards were on cue, but I had no clue as to how they would play out during the day's hike.

The Nagual wandered the immediate area, picking up rocks, pebbles, and stones. She handed one to every person in the group without saying a word. The rock she handed me filled my palm and the length of my fingers. It was a lava rock, maybe half a pound in weight. I gazed down at the rock in my hand. Everyone was doing the same with the rocks they held. Some had tiny pebbles no more than an inch in length, and some had even larger rocks than the one I now carried in my palm. Our two remaining group members arrived and we were ready to go.

Running parallel to the road was a potholed asphalt trail, which we began trudging up. It spanned the hillside from the road toward the ocean, a distance of a quarter mile, ascending as it went, and from a hiker's perspective it led right off the edge of the cliff into the ocean. But we weren't yet to the edge, and couldn't see where it made a hairpin turn at the top of the knoll leading to several WWII bunkers overlooking the eastern tip of the island. Over the edge of the trail was the cliffside we would soon be scrambling to negotiate. The older apprentices had already clued me in to the fact that the Nagual loved to hike the gargantuan boulders along the cliff with the ocean waves at their base pounding upon the rough, volcanic surface.

I walked along at a measured pace as I turned my gaze to the stone in my hand. I remembered what a Lakota Medicine Man by the name of Chief Phil Crazy Bull had told me during my sweat lodge days: "Rocks can give you full thought."[17] I wondered if the rock had any thought to give me. Just like the hike on Mauna Kea when the stones called out to me, I paid attention to my random thoughts. Paying attention to them was a way of being in a state of non-duality: thoughts arrived with purpose and had a role to play in the moment. It was for me to discover the reason for their appearance inside me.

Another hundred feet came and went. Turning to my right, I could see a huge lava boulder ahead and to the side of the trail. Flat and smooth on top, it was a resting spot for hikers coming both directions along the asphalt trail. Without a thought, I set my rock down, placing it on top of the natural lava bench. Glancing ahead, I hurried my pace to catch up with the Nagual and the group in front of me. Heart thumping, I realized that its accelerated rate wasn't due to the rise in elevation as we hiked along. The physical pounding of my heart was always a signpost to the center of my energetic being, even while dreaming at night. As though an afterthought, my mind went into gear: *What did I just do? What does the rock represent anyway? How long are we supposed to carry it? Will the Nagual notice? Does this have anything to do with aggressiveness and boundaries?* We continued hiking for a quarter mile while I continued my internal inquisition. Any internal silence I'd had when I set the rock down had momentarily taken wing. An odd thought suddenly came to me; a thought that I needed to pay attention to.

Carry the rock and not the weight of the rock, Jess.

That'd been the lesson long ago to the apprentices while balancing the women's different physical bodies with only the use of our fingers in the air. As we had lifted each woman, each one in turn had had very different energy that could be felt through our fingertips. We had learned that each person's perception of the weight she carried was different. That weight could either be weighed down or freed up depending on how it was viewed. The connection was clear. Here in this moment, I had carried a weight briefly then set it down – a rock that'd been handed to me by the Nagual. The distinction between having an experience as opposed to adding undue weight to that same experience flashed before me.

The Nagual stopped walking, allowing time for everyone to catch up to her. She pointed to several land markings along the trail: the rusted iron gate used in WWII to gain access to the bunkers, the telephone poles planted along the hillside with glass insulators still fixed on the cross-arms, the natural channel running alongside the road that occasionally flooded with seawater during storm tides.

With no segue in topic she abruptly turned to Linda and asked, "Where's your stone?" Linda pointed to her backpack. "I put it here for safekeeping."

"You need to carry it in your hands," the Nagual said. Linda looked surprised. No one had said anything about what to do or not to do with the stones that had been handed us. As Linda shifted her backpack to pull out her stone, the Nagual looked around. Seeing my hands at my sides, sans a stone like Linda, she asked, "Where's your rock?"

I didn't hesitate a moment. "I set it down," I admitted. The group of hikers around us stood stock-still. No one moved. For a brief instant in time, my words had come out faster than my thought process. I didn't know why I'd set the rock down; therefore I wasn't able to explain my actions to the Nagual. In the next moment, I realized that I had just said no to the Nagual's directive.

"You need to go get it," the Nagual directed.

I answered evenly, although the pounding inside my chest could have drowned the sound of ocean waves on the beach. "No." I didn't have time to think through what was happening, but it was a moment of clear Intent and non-duality. All of me – everything about my life up to this moment and forever after – would be impacted by this moment of clarity and action represented by saying, "No."

My next statement sounded absurd under the circumstances, and was my thought process kicking in. I blurted out, "Maybe this is where aggressiveness and boundaries comes in," as though my job was to provide a play-by-play commentary of what was happening. I had taken on the role of actress in a scene never played before and had switched over to audience critic in milliseconds.

"You need to go get your stone." The Nagual was resolute.

"No," I repeated. The resignation in my voice was as final as was her next statement.

"Then you cannot continue on the hike."

To deny the Nagual's request was unplanned, as was setting the stone down in the first place. It was action unmediated by thought and desire; it was pure Intent. The Nagual looked impassive; as though her heart had nary skipped a beat but remained steady regardless of what was taking place between us.

I didn't dare look at the other apprentices standing around me, but I could feel the tension in the group from my refusal to do what the Nagual directed me to do. No one spoke a word as though they were holding the tension of the moment just before it burst asunder. The Nagual kept her eyes on me and waited.

Turning to Barbara I asked, "Will you be able to get a ride home?" Barbara appealed to the group and someone quickly offered her a ride home after the day's hike. Without saying another word, I turned away from the Nagual. The group was silent, although if body posture could speak it would've been a high-pitched squeal for as awkward as everyone looked. The movie scene had just jettisoned to an unfamiliar locale with unscripted material, and no one knew the lines.

My mind continued to be blank but my awareness was big. Inside my mind, physical space opened up as though a car reversed out of its spot in a crowded parking lot. This phenomenon was not unique to me; it is our birthright when we are free of beliefs, values, thoughts, and emotions. The awareness that I had arrived at an unadulterated moment of freedom hit me like an unexpected punch to the jaw – square, solid, and hard. I stopped walking to absorb the shock.

In an instant, as though it were the moment before death, my time with the Nagual flashed before my eyes:

I move to Hawaii to study with a Toltec Nagual. She invites me to be her apprentice. I attend every single event she offers, despite the agitation I often feel while with her. I study with her to the best of my ability and now, just moments ago, I tell her, "No"; I refuse do what she is asking of me.

There was no emotion involved in saying "No." It wasn't about an emotional reaction; it was a spontaneous moment of truth.

I also realized that the Nagual had acted in the manner she had, and I had acted in the manner I had, and even though the two acts looked like an uncompromising face-off, they had been equal acts. Never before had I realized how much "yes" and "no" were the same. They were equal acts! Neither one had priority or precedence over the other. Badger and Armadillo – different, yet the same.

Then another awareness was delivered, like a one-two double jab: "Don't put morality onto what happened. That's not what's happening here." It was the voice inside my head that was not my mind. It was my higher consciousness telling me that saying "No" was an act of freedom and self-direction as opposed to an act of resistance and refusal.

At once I felt light as a feather! A tremendous feeling of freedom and lightness permeated my being. I walked down the trail to the huge lava rock where I'd placed the smaller stone ages before – a millennium in time, it seemed. Picking up the stone, I put it back in the palm of my hand and sat down.

Precious few thoughts were in the warehouse of my mind, making it plain to see what was located in the vastness of its space. Very clearly I could delineate between the thoughts that had morality in them and the free thoughts, brand new for me because they were outside my familiar inventory of thinking. I asked the stone in the palm of my hand what had happened.

"It was as necessary for you to say 'No'," the stone answered, "as it was necessary for the Nagual to say, 'Go.'" I felt free, weightless, and without thought in that moment of vast consequences that Intent had inexplicably drawn me into.

Stepping into the innocence and trust of my own growth and maturity was the lesson in the South on the medicine wheel. Tempting as it was to berate myself for saying what I did and for not following the Nagual's directions, the lesson was in taking responsibility for the direction of my own life on every level – spiritually, psychologically, emotionally, and energetically – even when the fallout included loss and confusion. Resistance – if my "No" could be labeled as such – had come just moments before one of the biggest breakthroughs of my life, just as the Nagual taught.

September 8

"Interesting choice yesterday," the Nagual commented, as she lay down on the massage table Saturday morning. I had set up the massage table and fitted the sheets without saying a word. On the drive to the Nagual's place, I had told myself that if there were a discussion between us about the events the previous day, I would describe what had happened rather than defend my position.

I didn't want to assume that I was wrong for not carrying the rock, for looking as though I'd defied what she'd instructed me to do, because I knew my actions indicated something very different. However, I lacked confidence that I could explain my actions. I always strove for language to describe experience, but for once language couldn't describe what had happened on the previous day. My actions had been independent of thought, so how could I explain them to the Nagual? From my perspective, however, those actions had been generated from a state of non-duality.

I began to work on the Nagual, at first lightly spreading the oil from my hands over the length of her back, then concentrating on the shoulders, adding pressure as the muscles relaxed under the effleurage. After the weird turn of events of the day before, I'd had the rest of the day to question and doubt myself about my refusal to pick up my rock. The freedom I felt after saying no to the Nagual, the conviction of "right action," had slowly been replaced by self-judgment, and I had already raked myself over the coals for even uttering the word.

I went over the events in my mind: I attended a group hiking event, was handed a rock to carry, set the rock down, was told the hike was off limits unless I retrieved the rock, and then I left the activity because I was not willing to go and get the rock after I'd set it down. But looking at the events themselves didn't satisfactorily explain what had taken place.

What remained amidst all of the uncertainty was the absolute sense of freedom after I'd said no to the Nagual. The purity of that feeling didn't coincide with the events themselves, not in my mind; but I could no more explain the incident to the Nagual, nor my rationale nor thought process, with any greater degree of understanding this morning than I had been able to yesterday. I finally spoke up in an effort to explain.

"When I walked away yesterday," I said, "I was profoundly aware of how differently we both viewed what had happened. I could grasp your position as clearly as I could grasp my own. From your perspective I was being willful and resistant. From my perspective I was stepping into my own Power. Neither of our positions was right or wrong. We had two very different experiences of the same event." Speaking carefully, I wanted to convey the juxtaposition of our positions. It was the Nagual's turn to be quiet.

Tentatively, as though she was testing her hypothesis aloud, she said, "It's interesting to me because, for the longest time, I didn't feel I had permission to push on you, and when I finally did, you responded by saying, 'No.'"

Instantly a memory surfaced of walking up to the Nagual after that evening lecture months ago. Her talk that evening which had been about her intention to ask more from all the apprentices because she'd been too lax on everyone. Nonplussed by her declaration of toughening up, I'd said to her, "You have permission! Push on me in whatever way you feel is needed." Interesting, that she didn't remember this. It had been yet another dialogue between us that had missed its intended target.

"There is a possibility that I got the push you meant, but not in the way you think. Both of us simply have a different perspective of events. The response of 'yes' and 'no' hold equal energy but their meaning is viewed differently by each of us."

As my hands moved down her lower back and onto her hips, I worked silently, although the silence was pregnant because the conversation had not yet crowned. I pondered how the Nagual's story of my resistance paralleled my story of her resistance to letting me work on her hip. Again and again I had invited her to do deeper work, and again and again I had not gotten an affirmative response.

"You know, there is more work that can be done on this hip, and yet we've never done it," I said. The Nagual lay quietly. I worked for a while longer without saying more. Internally, a thought was straining against being spoken by the picket line of my lips. I longed to say, "Tell me more about your perspective of what happened yesterday," but I stopped myself. If I asked her for her perspective on my actions, I would be handing over my actions for approval, and hadn't I just experienced the freedom in having not done that? It was the very thing the other apprentices did too freely with the Nagual; they expected her to do their thinking for them. I wanted to think through the experience on my own, to feel it, to accept it from the core of who I was rather than hearing her interpretation of what had happened.

Lifting one of her hands into my own, I began to knead it gently. All of the Nagual's energy was in her hands. I'd noticed this before, and here it was again. Feeling as though an electrical current was charging through them, they felt warm, pulsing with life. "Your hands hold all of the energy in your body; they're supercharged," I observed aloud.

"I was told a long time ago that I would do energetic healing. Somehow, it ties in with doing emotional and energetic release work. I'm not quite sure how. It's been coming up more than ever in the past few months. I did a lot of energy work on the hike yesterday, so it makes sense that you feel the energy there."

I was astounded at what the Nagual said! Not only had she shared something intimate with me in regards to who she was, but I felt strongly that there was a link that tied together two seemingly disparate experiences. Her energetic work done during yesterday's hike was linked with the energetic work we'd been doing together for the past six months. I was sure of it! This was the principle Bruce had taught me while doing energetic bodywork, that the body doesn't lie. In addition, the Nagual had taught me that, "There is no out there."

The Nagual just disclosed that the energy in her hands had been used to do energy work, when years ago she'd been unable to access those same healing abilities. I had always been clear as to my own abilities while doing massage work, and now it felt like my work on her for the past six months had impacted her own abilities at energetic healing! There it was! The work we'd been doing for the past six months was paying off! I hesitated to make that connection for the Nagual, as she wasn't appearing to make it for herself. Due to the huge shift of my assemblage point yesterday (i.e. the "empty parking spot"), I was seeing things I'd never noticed before.

Working on the Nagual necessitated that I do the bodywork in a manner I was unfamiliar with. The work done was without any verbal processing whatsoever. But doing the work differently didn't mean nothing was taking place. As a therapist, I valued talking through issues, concerns, and problems even while doing bodywork, because that's what my training and experience had been. I placed a high value on "talking" through the experience between masseuse and client. Regarding the massage work, I placed less value on the work alone than if we'd been having a verbal exchange at the same time. Ah! What an oversight!

Maybe the Nagual processed internally without having the need to say anything to me. Maybe verbal processing wasn't important to her in the same way it was to me. Even though she'd said no to specific work on her hip, the work we had done had improved her healing abilities.

What the Nagual had just disclosed to me was an open door too good to be true. I stepped through. "Didn't you say that the Nagual that you worked with did emotional work while doing massage work?"

"Yes, and for some reason I objected to it. Maybe I wasn't quite ready for it yet," she acknowledged. She made no verbal connection between how she approached massage and the fact that the body tells a story regardless of whether or not the person on the table is able or willing to acknowledge it. This was the very point I had hesitated to make for her, yet here it was between us yet again.

"I've asked myself over and over about your hip. I've indicated to you that it needs work done on it. What's the reason we haven't done it? Whose responsibility is it to take the initiative and to go into the work? Is it the client's or the massage therapist's?"

The questions were not meant to be rhetorical. Had she ever wrestled in this way with her work with the apprentices? I often had these same questions while doing psychotherapy. Was my job to lead the client, to push them from behind, or was walking alongside the best approach? Had I driven my point home to the Nagual? Had I been tactful or painfully blunt?

Now the Nagual remained quiet. I completed the massage. The Nagual's cat, drawn to the energy swirling around the massage table, had found a comfortable spot between the Nagual's knees during the later part of the massage. I brought my hand to the cat's nose, asking permission to touch her. She pushed her nose into my fingers and I rubbed her head. Petting this cat was by invitation only; she'd let you know with a bat of her claws whether or not she wanted you to touch her.

The Nagual opened her eyes. "You know, we can take our relationship to the next level if you want."

"What does that mean?" I blurted out with an intensity of hopefulness and longing that surprised me. Her comment was unexpected and it sounded promising, an invitation to move the relationship between us into a different direction, a direction in which there was clearer and more open communication.

"I don't know. Let's find out," she said. Rising off the table, the Nagual reached for her clothes. The cat objected to the loss of her comfy position with a screech and leapt to the floor. I walked to the kitchen to wash the massage oil from my hands.

If only the Nagual meant that we could give ourselves more opportunity for dialogue that didn't always feel like it was loaded with obscure and indefinite comments, I would jump at the invitation. If only the Nagual meant that we could carry on with give-and-take, mutually supportive conversation between us. But as usual, I didn't know clearly what her statement meant, and if I asked for clarification, my questions would be received as a challenge to her authority, just as I'd felt so often when making comments during discussions after her Tuesday and Thursday lectures. Any dialogue we had between us tired me out and I was never sure as to the reason why.

September 12

Driving to work on the Monday after the aborted hike with the Nagual I didn't feel well at all. Within half an hour of stepping into the office door my throat began to tickle. I felt tightness and tension in my neck. My eyes bulged from their sockets due to the pressure in my head. My lower back throbbed. I started coughing. It was the kind of coughing that seemed endless like the drip on a leaky faucet. Disoriented and miserable, I went home halfway through the day and fell onto the bed like a dead (wo)man. I didn't move, lying in bed feverish and forlorn.

The next day the flu continued to dog me, but I couldn't "not" go to class Tuesday evening. I'd not missed one Tuesday or Thursday evening in the entire time I'd been an apprentice, and with all that had happened over the previous few days, that night was not the time to start. Yet, on this evening during the Nagual's teaching time, I hit a wall. I hadn't seen it coming, and suddenly I felt myself slam into a brick barrier at full speed while my body sat quietly on the carpet during the Nagual's lecture. I became exhausted listening to her go on about her animals, her own apprenticeship, and her projects. She wouldn't put up with hearing as much about any one of our children or pets as often as we heard about her dog.

Was I feeling resistant? Guilty! Maggots were crawling all over the carcass of my apprenticeship with the Nagual.

For too long I had wondered why in the hell we weren't able to communicate with each other any better than we did. For too long I had watched her responses to the other apprentices and been appalled. With Barb she was patronizing, and with Carol, cajoling. She coddled Liz, was almost respectful with Suzanne, and with Barbara she was bored. I was treated with indifference – at least that's what I felt from her. I couldn't get these thoughts out of my head. They were heavy and weighed me down with ugliness.

There was no way to talk about it all with the Nagual. To question her was forbidden. Like talking in a family about Mom or Dad being drunk, or the fact that there are half-empty liquor bottles hidden throughout the house. Those topics are impossible to talk about in an alcoholic family! Everyone is forbidden to speak of the giant pachyderm in the room. Which leads me to a list of rules that were unspoken but, which the group abided by. I'd seen them played out over and over:

1. Ideas on the Toltec path other than the Nagual's ideas were forbidden; never was there a time to share social Toltec discourse.
2. There was a bevy of acceptable language; deviation was only acceptable within certain limits.
3. Ask questions but don't question.
4. The story was the Nagual's to tell; eventually everyone else told the same tale.
5. The cook didn't have to play by the same rules; let's not notice the double standards.
6. The Nagual's childhood stories were fascinating and we wanted to hear more.
7. We should all have the same values the Nagual does, including the importance of watering the palms every evening after meditation.
8. Resistance was when you said no to the Nagual.

Bitter, bitter, bitter. How long had I been choking on these bitter herbs and telling myself all the while they were sweet peppermint! Had everyone agreed to play the same game? The power of group dynamics came back to me: all of us were reacting to the unspoken dynamics occurring before our eyes without challenging those very group rules!

Crow had told me clearly, "Stay here a while. It'll be good for you." The lavender stone had told me clearly, "Don't abandon yourself to anything." Intent had told me clearly, "Finish your book by the end of the year." The Nagual had told me clearly, "You're resistant and fearful."

The Nagual measured the success of her apprentices by how she was as an apprentice. Her apprenticeship had lasted three years, and she'd been there every time the door was opened without fail. "I saw hundreds of people go through the Temple but only a handful made it," she often told us. What in the hell did that sentence imply? If attendance was the measure of an apprentice's performance, I'd get an "A;" but it wasn't about getting to class on time, it was something else, something I couldn't quite put my finger on.

There was so much that was unclear between us! But I couldn't deny that I expected our massage work to fall in line with my previous massage work – just as the Nagual expected her apprentices to benefit from completing the same activities she'd done with her teacher. Both of us were measuring one experience with the template of a former experience, like expecting a second-born child to be the mirror image of a firstborn sibling.

I was done. Weary. Heartbroken. For me, at that particular moment, which was 2:25am, I had done my time, all nine months of it. The result: full term, live birth. And it would be life on my own for a while. We'd see if the New Year brought with it any desire to return to the fold.

September 14

My daughter, Carla, was trying to help me sort it all out over the phone.

"Mom, you're confusing what happened between you and the Nagual by attributing judgment to her that is really your own. Remember Byron Katie? You didn't like getting the two cards, Armadillo and Badger (two very secret animals by the way), and you carried your dislike of those animal characteristics to the encounter with the Nagual.

"You said 'No' to her. That's reality. You weren't simply saying 'No' about the hike and about the energy exchange during massage. You were saying 'No' to her as your teacher."

The phone conversation was painful, like a sucker punch to my gut. It knocked the wind right out of me. But I needed to hear every word Carla uttered. The timing was perfect. Doesn't mean it was easy to hear. It was agonizing to hear my actions described so blatantly and then to face the ramifications of those actions.

I had shared with Carla everything that had gone down between the Nagual and me, and she was stripping me of all the shoring up I'd been working diligently at over the previous week to strengthen my point of view. And that shoring up had something to do with guilt.

"You're struggling with your own idea about what it means to have a teacher," she went on. "Did you ever consider, really, that you don't need a teacher? None of us do, although some of us tell ourselves we do. That's what you've done. I don't hear judgment or resistance in what you're telling me she said. And she's said 'No' to your offer to do more work on her hip. There's no reason to take offense. Saying 'No' doesn't imply judgment, remember? And, if you notice, it's an example of spirit's irony: you and the Nagual said the same thing to each other."

"No! No! No!" reverberated in my head, over and over. It was as though a warning system had been triggered and was blaring repeatedly. Once a month throughout the year, tsunami warnings sounded across the island. Initially, I would panic as though they were signaling a real tsunami, when they were merely the first of the month testing of the island's warning system. Carla, on the other hand, was suggesting that my "No" had been more than merely not hiking the cliffside. My "No" had included saying no to her as a teacher.

Carla's voice softened. "Mom, it sounds as though your energy and the Nagual's energy are not similar enough to work together. Besides, the Nagual doesn't have the only avenue to learn the Toltec path, much as you wanted her to. She has one way, but it's not the only way. Separate 'her way' from 'her way is best.'"

"You projected your own judgment of the experience onto her and then, like a boomerang, turned it back on yourself by getting the flu. Free yourself of that point of view. Don't attribute judgment, a yes or no, to either one of you. Both were necessary, which is exactly what the rock told you!"

I had wanted a teacher, a mentor, a guru, a Nagual – all of those attributes locked down into one individual. That was the preferred method when one studied an art, a philosophy, a belief system, a path, a different cognition. The education, the learning, the experiences were conducted between student and teacher. It had been inconceivable to me that the Nagual and I weren't a good match for each other; therefore I simply hadn't seen our incompatibility.

The first time I'd met the Nagual she'd told me, "To be on this path you need a Nagual." I'd bought into that belief hook, line, and sinker. Everything I'd read led me to believe that to go further on the Toltec path required a Nagual. And the Nagual had been an apprentice in the past and was now offering her expertise to students. But I had never considered the possibility that the Nagual or the apprentice would err in their decision to work with each other. It wasn't in my Toltec belief system.

Was a Nagual and apprentice relationship the only method for teaching Toltec knowledge? Was I in any position to question the efficacy of the ancient tradition? Was there room for a paradigm shift in how the knowledge was passed on? And if there were, what would it look like? Those questions were beginning to poke through stony ground, but I was nowhere near to answering them.

Carla continued, "You put yourself into an untenable position, wanting, desiring, believing in a teacher to the exclusion of yourself. Then all along you denied what you knew because you had a teacher who you expected to do the teaching."

"The untenable position was that you expected her to teach, and you were teaching yourself at the same time, something that was not all right with you. Your attention was misplaced. Your expectations were misaligned. You didn't believe you could listen to her and to yourself at the same time, did you? Part of the reason for your confusion is the implication for being your own teacher, a position you didn't believe in for yourself, or your beliefs for being without a teacher, which implied that you didn't deserve a teacher in the first place. Neither one of those positions was acceptable to you. You believed along with the Nagual that the only way to progress was to apprentice with a Nagual. What you've found is that's simply not true for you." Her words were naked truth staring me in the face.

January 7

For the next four months I had no contact with the Nagual or her other apprentices. On this morning, I had a dream about the apprenticeship. It had shown up from left field, like a teakettle whistling on a stovetop. You know the kettle is on, but when the whistle blows your mind has been elsewhere and so the whistling takes you by surprise. I had put the apprenticeship on hold until the end of the year based on what Crow had advised. It had been in the back of my mind, waiting. I knew that the apprenticeship was going to do one of three things: resume, evolve, or come to an end, but I didn't know which one was going to occur.

In the dream, I join an outing with the Nagual and a group of apprentices. We are at the end of our time together. Seems we've had a sleepover in a travel trailer as celebration. As I look around to gather my things, I can't find two items that belong to me: my bra and my watch. I rifle through everyone's clothing, scattered on the floor, to look for my belongings. Clothes are strewn everywhere, just like at a real life sleepover.

The Nagual asks us to choose ceramic items from a large bin. They are going to be used as an object for the day's lesson. I choose a large conch shell that has a collection of smaller shells nestled inside its pink underside. All of the ceramics are chipped or have cracks. We look them over curiously. I am irritated that they appear to be items that have been poorly cared for.

A huge tsunami swells to gargantuan size in the distance. Just before the wall of water drops on top of us, I bolt to higher ground, followed closely by several others in the group. The Nagual doesn't budge from her seat. A short time later I look up. Where is that tsunami? The green wave towering above us has not fallen; but as I look closely, I see that it has transformed instead into a green sky. I return to find the Nagual seated in the same position she'd been in before.

The dream had unfolded in the early morning hours while in a state of gnosis. I was curious about it and became convinced the dream was a prompt to go see the Nagual. It just so happened that this was a Tuesday, a night on which the Nagual met with her apprentices on a weekly basis. I decided I'd drop by to say hi to everyone. I remembered that on occasion other people used to drop in at the Center when I was in attendance, so no need to worry about whether or not it was kosher.

The past few months had been busy. Busy with writing and busy at work, because I'd been transferred from Program II to Program III, and that, in and of itself, had amped up the time and attention I devoted to doing my job. The "busy-ness" had also allowed me to look elsewhere so that I was not having to look directly at the apprenticeship and what had occurred. Looking directly at it had proven so far to be too painful.

An hour before class time, I began to doubt why I was going to class. Early that morning the dream omen had been so clear and direct; one of those events that compelled me to "right action." But as the actual time of the meeting grew near, I began to lose my resolve. The certainty I'd had early in the morning had been watered down with worry.

Don't put yourself under pressure to know the reasons you might be going, I cautioned myself. *When you awoke from the dream with the conclusion to stop by the Center, you were certain of that decision. Go! Whether or not you understand the reasons for going.* The sense of urgency was intense as though the urgency itself would paddle through the thick sea of anxiety it was floating in.

I arrived at the Center shortly before 7:00pm, minutes before the Nagual usually started her evening talk. Barbara, Linda, Julie, and Barb greeted me. The greetings felt genuine and warm, although the casual atmosphere soon turned sticky. Several of the women began to look around, watching for the Nagual to appear. One person asked if I was staying for the evening. Another asked if the Nagual knew I was coming. The apprentices were looking around covertly as though they expected they would have to answer to the Nagual for why I was standing in their midst. And because I wasn't clear on why I was there, I couldn't explain to anyone else why I was there.

For a few short minutes, we stood in gridlock, waiting for someone to push through the discomfort. Movement in the hallway caught my eye. The Nagual exited the bathroom and walked the short distance to her office. In those few steps she looked over at the entryway and made eye contact with me. I saw that she saw me, and then she continued walking into her office. I excused myself and walked down the hallway to the Nagual's office door. It was open. She was standing in front of her desk looking at paperwork in her hand. I had the feeling she'd been waiting for me to walk in.

"I hope it's okay that I dropped by tonight," I said as I walked over to her and gave her a hug.

"Well, it's actually not a good time," replied the Nagual. "We're in the middle of a process, and tonight is the end of that process. But you can come on Thursday if you'd like. Then I go to Mexico for three weeks. Maybe you can stop back by in February if you're not able to make it on Thursday."

"Okay, thanks, I'm not able to make it on Thursday," I mumbled. I already knew I had a work commitment that evening and would be unable to attend the Nagual's class. I turned and walked out of her office. There didn't seem to be any more to say between us. I also knew I didn't have the courage to return. It had taken all I had to walk in the door fifteen minutes earlier. By now the group of women had moved into the main meeting area, and were seated on the carpet waiting for the Nagual. I grabbed my shoes by the front door and walked out.

No doubt now, I thought to myself as I reached inside my purse for my car keys. *It's over.*

My apprenticeship had truly come to an end. In the back of my mind, over the previous months, there had been a little trapdoor that was going to allow me to join the group again, to be the apprentice without question, the apprentice that followed all directives, the apprentice that never said, "No."

But as it turned out, that apprentice wasn't me. Maybe someone else, but not me.

In a secret Armadillo and Badger kind of way, I had wanted to return at the beginning of the New Year to resume my apprenticeship. After the awkwardness that night, I knew it wasn't going to happen in a million years. As a therapist, I had helped people resolve their relationship problems. That was my job. If it wasn't resolution they wanted, we tried to figure out what they did want. Some people wanted to talk, some people wanted to blame, some people wanted to figure out and understand. I'd looked at the apprenticeship for the past few months in the same way. My relationship with the Nagual needed resolution, and for the life of me, I had tried to figure it out. I had wanted to talk, even to blame, and to understand. Above all, I had had hope we could work things out between us.

But my journey with the Nagual was over. There wasn't going to be a redo. I looked at the dream carefully. In it was a message of transformation, even closure that I missed seeing earlier in the morning.

A slumber party is a time for fun, a time of joining and cohabiting, of partying and playing, of learning and exploring. I believed I'd had that, if only briefly, with the Nagual as her apprentice. There'd been good times between us. A bra symbolizes support and protection – sometimes too much protection – and I'd lost it somewhere along the way.[18] A wristwatch signifies structure, the structure of one's thoughts, expectations, and adherence to life in incremental doses. That was also gone. Both of those objects had disappeared during the overnight slumber party.

A good thing, I concluded. Too much protection dampened free movement. When one loses a sense of time, it's because they've been involved and engaged; they haven't been checking their watch as an expression of boredom or disconnect.

I'd been looking for those items in the dream precisely because I'd been able to let them go. My feelings during the slumber party had not been distraught but lighthearted and free.

Similar in interpretation to the bra, seashells symbolized security and the act of protection. In fact, their meaning leaned toward hiding or protecting the true self and real feelings. Hadn't I told myself again and again, "Don't become involved; remove yourself from the dynamics of what goes on between everyone"? In an effort not to become too involved in the group dynamics, I had protected myself rather than shared about myself. My stance had been to put all my energy into grasping the Nagual's teachings rather than building relationships.

A tsunami is the symbol for overwhelming or repressed feeling. For the past few months, I had been missing the Nagual and the other apprentices. At times, the sadness had been intense and stemmed from the loss of my connection to them. Despite having placed my attention on the teachings and interactions with the Nagual, I was aware that I was grieving the loss of those relationships and also grieving the loss of being an apprentice.

A tsunami occurs with little warning. It is sudden and brings intense, destructive change. But this dream tsunami had not been your usual tsunami, starting with its green color, and it was there that the dream had brought a sense of healing and vigor, peace and serenity, because the tsunami hadn't actually overwhelmed those in the dream. Instead, it had transformed into a green sky over our heads of high hopes and possibilities.

The Nagual hadn't changed her position throughout the dream, although I had changed mine. She may have handed out what I perceived to be chipped and cracked goods, but I had been the one to choose a secure and protective shell, no different than a turtle that pulls into its carapace at the sight or sound of danger. In the dream, I had been the one to run in the opposite direction whereas the Nagual had stayed put. Furthermore, I understood that for the Nagual, there may never have been a tsunami in the first place. It was my experience after all, not hers.

A month came and went and then I received an e-mail from the Nagual. She wrote: "I have thought of you often and of our relationship. I have avoided telling you that I can't be your teacher. You are more than welcome to touch bases, but I can't stand in the role of teacher for you. What role I can play I am not sure, but teacher is clearly not it." My apprenticeship was officially over.

The end of the apprenticeship was the beginning of trust in myself to sustain my own journey forward. South on the medicine wheel is the direction of passion, fullness, and self-direction. It is the direction of releasing the past and walking softly on the earth. I was on my way to embracing the freedom those energies would bring to my life.

Epilogue

When I had flown to Hawaii to begin my apprenticeship with the Nagual, I had been certain that she would take me as an apprentice regardless of the apprenticeship not being official before I arrived. That's the evidence of Intent in one's life. What I hadn't seen ahead of me was the future of that relationship, and how it would play out between us. That's not a bad thing. Future events are an energetic anomaly because they don't exist anyway. Arriving on the doorstep of the Nagual's centre had been "in the cards," a period of time in which our lives converged with Intent exactly as both of us intended. What I made of the opportunity is the story you've just read.

Had I been more aware of what my expectations were, had I been more aware that I would put the Nagual on a pedestal and she would come crashing down, had I been more aware that "relationship" was a bigger part of an apprenticeship than I had anticipated, I might have approached things differently. The Nagual had a saying: "Argue for your limitations and they're yours." Even though I've told my side of the story, I recognize others involved may have a very different perspective. I've said my piece, and I recognize in the telling that it is only one slice of the proverbial pie.

Neither does it serve anyone involved, in this instance me, to "explain away" an experience, in effect to answer for every nuance that occurred. Author Carol Proudfoot-Edgar said that, "When we talk too long and too often about our experiences, we diminish the magic and make them ordinary."[19] My apprenticeship was anything but ordinary, and I'm grateful for every moment I spent with the Nagual.

Since my apprenticeship with the Nagual, multitudes of global workshops, conferences, online apprenticeships, forums, even blogs, have exploded with accessibility related to the Toltec path. After my time with the Nagual, I went on to be involved in several forums related to the Toltec path, traveled abroad to study with other teachers, and built ongoing relationships in the global Toltec community. These aspects of being "live" are difficult to duplicate if the contact is limited to electronic formatting as a means of developing a relationship. Even though I was aware during my apprenticeship that the Nagual had online students, I considered it a privilege to study with her face to face.

Suggestions for those of you who are interested in experiencing a face-to-face apprenticeship include the following.

Follow Intent. All else will fall into place. Intent is a guiding force in the Universe that is analogous to a mighty river. Once you locate the river's edge by being aware that your life is larger than your individual story, once you step into this vital, uncompromising flow, allowing it to direct your actions, then the precise people, place, and perspective to suit you WILL become the movement of the river. From there, you're on your way. Whether or not the experience turns out the way you hoped, expected, or even desired, is inconsequential to what will take place. That is the mystery of being in the movement of Intent. My Intent was to be in a face-to-face apprenticeship with a Toltec Nagual, and that's exactly what I got!

Be aware that if all of the nuances of the journey could be seen ahead of time, that in itself would diminish the journey, and that's not what you want. Be open to the unknown, the unfamiliar, and the untried.

Others may not be of a mind to relocate across the Pacific Ocean without careful planning and meticulous details, in hopes of making the journey as smooth as possible with minimal bumps in the road. For example, moving to a new location, without a job waiting, may not be everyone's *kuleana* (Hawaiian for "mode of operating"). Whereas for me it was "right action," since I was confident in acquiring a position that would fit Intent once I arrived in Hawaii.

Know yourself well enough to know how your personality and character traits may influence your journey and be open to change them. I was adamant that I had come to study with the Nagual rather than to form friendships, single-minded in my devotion to "studying" with the Nagual. Picture a kid who has her nose in a textbook during recess while the rest of the kids are playing jump rope. What might have been different had I been more open? If I had been more open to differences, I would have been less annoyed when the Nagual suggested, "Go down to the mall and people watch" (i.e. expand your horizons and your way of being in the world).

Trust in the moment rather than hold it up to a yardstick of "truth." The only template I had for what an apprenticeship "looked like" was reading Carlos Castaneda. I might as well have whacked myself across the fingers with a ruler, not once but consistently, for as often as I compared my experience with his apprenticeship. Millions have done the same thing, I know, and yet I fell for doing it too. Making those (erroneous) comparisons is one of the major factors for telling my story here, i.e. "Don't do what I did; do it differently." The passing on of knowledge is in the moment of the experience, *not* in how it compares to someone else's experiences. To compare is a buzzkill at the highest level.

Look for what happens once you are seated with a teacher, and not at what doesn't happen. This has more to do with where you place your attention than on making comparisons. I veered way too close to labeling the apprenticeship a "failure" because I had such difficulty communicating with the Nagual, as though communication was the sine qua non of the entire experience! Yet when I look at what took place on an overt level, the Nagual provided consistent teachings/lecture, techniques, activities, special events, and access with others of like mind. On an energetic level, she provided loads of experience and expertise in working with and accessing non-physical realms.

In the end the Nagual and I gave the same thing to each other. We gave our time and attention, our expertise as teacher and student, and we shared our distinctly different energy with each other. At the end of the day, my "yes" had changed to "no," and in that there was no harm, nor foul. As a maxim, "There is no out there" became my reality with major elements to my experience being the death of ideals, a nascent life of expanded awareness, and a forward evolution into the non-duality of daily life. In the end, the rock became weightless and free of encumbrance.

Endnotes

1. Jessica Rzeszewski, *Encounter with Power: A Journey from the Toltec Perspective* (British Columbia: Trafford Publishing, 2013)
2. Arnold Mindell, *The Shaman's Body: A New Shamanism for Transforming Health, Relationships, and the Community* (New York: HarperCollins Publishers, 1993), 52
3. Robert Monroe, *Far Journeys* (New York: Doubleday & Company, 1987), 77
4. *A.I. Artificial Intelligence,* directed by Steven Spielberg. United States: Warner Brothers, 2001
5. Byron Katie, *Loving What Is* (New York: Three Rivers Press, 2002), 19
6. Erich Schiffman, *Yoga: The Spirit and Practice of Moving into Stillness* (New York: Simon & Shuster, 1996), 53
7. Tomas, *The Promise of Power: Reflections on the Toltec Warriors' Dialogue from the Collected Works of Carlos Castaneda* (Virginia: Hampton Roads Publishing Company, 1995), 559
8. Monroe, *Far Journeys*
9. Matthew 6:28, *Bible* (King James Version)
10. Carlos Castaneda, *The Art of Dreaming* (New York: HarperCollins Publishers, 1993)
11. Ibid., 234
12. Ibid., 164
13. Carlos Castaneda, *The Teachings of Don Juan: A Yaqui Way of Knowledge* (Los Angeles: University of California Press, 1968)
14. Jamie Sams and David Carson, *Medicine Cards* (New York: St. Martin's Press, 1988)
15. Ibid., 149
16. Ibid., 153
17. Chief Phil Crazy Bull, lecture for "Sacred Teachings of the Lakota Way of Life," Los Angeles, May 6, 2000

18. See "Dream Moods," http://www.dreammoods.com. Interpretations for dream.
19. Carol Proudfoot-Edgar, conversation with the author/shaman, August 1997.

MOON BOOKS

Moon Books invites you to begin or deepen your encounter with Paganism, in all its rich, creative, flourishing forms.